One of the strongest words that churches these days is that He wants to bless all His people with prosperity. Brian Sauder is hearing this word more clearly than most, and he has done a superb job of communicating it to us, chapter by chapter, in A Practical Path to a Properous Life. The richer you are, the more potential you have to advance God's kingdom in a significant way. This book not only gives theory but also practical steps toward experiencing prosperity in your own life.
—**C. Peter Wagner,** Vice-President, Global Spheres, Inc.

I have known Brian for many years, and his heart for transforming the body of Christ in the area of wealth management comes through on every page of this manuscript. After reading Brian's book, I'm confident it will help many believers. The included study questions provide practical applications for individuals and small group settings.
—***Dave Yarnes,*** Vice President, MorningStar Ministries
Founder of the Kingdom Business Association

With world economies shaking and personal financial securities under threat, this book from Brian Sauder is not only challenging and instructional, but timely. Third John 2 is John's prayer for Gaius: "Beloved, I pray that you may prosper in all things and be in health, just as your soul prospers." This prayer includes spirit, soul and body—the whole man—which includes our financial status. Brian provides a practical approach on the subject: One that will inspire you not only to experience a greater level of personal prosperity but also position you to be a blessing to many.
—**Tony Fitzgerald,** Apostolic Team Leader
Church of the Nations

What a timely book for the era in which we are living. The information in this book is instrumental to both wealth creation and wealth preservation. I have known Brian for a number of years, have read his previous book **Prosperity with a Purpose** *and appreciate how practical he is in life. I consider him to be a person of integrity who has concern for people's welfare. This book is an awesome tool for study and certainly empowering. Brian deals with the very thing that kills our drive and creativity—the spirit of poverty. Many people are actually afraid of wealth and would rather be poor. Read this book. I believe it will be a blessing to you.*

—Eugene Strite
Business Leader/Author/Speaker

With so much tension about money and how we manage it, Brian does a great job defusing the myths of poverty and wealth. But what I love most is Brian's practical approach toward our attitudes and actions in leveraging our resources for the kingdom of God.

—Phil Carnuccio
Pastor Providence Church/Leader Sequoia International

A Practical Path to a Prosperous Life

A Guide to Experiencing Prosperity with a Purpose

Brian Sauder

House to House Publications
www.h2hp.com

A Practical Path to a Prosperous Life

A Guide to Experiencing Prosperity with a Purpose

by Brian Sauder

© 2013 by Brian Sauder

Published by
House to House Publications
11 Toll Gate Road, Litiz, PA, USA
Tele: 717.627.1996
www.h2hp.com

ISBN: 978-1-886973-98-5

Printed in the United States of America

Contents

Appendix

Foreword

I have waited a long time for this book to be published. *A Practical Path to a Prosperous Life* is a revelation on finances that every Christian in our day desperately needs to understand and practice. This book will serve as a major tool in the hand of our God to train the present and coming generations in a biblical understanding of kingdom finances. But the book does not stop there. *A Practical Path to a Prosperous Life* also serves as a practical textbook so that God's people can actually experience the biblical revelation found in this book. This is a brilliant book!

A Practical Path to a Prosperous Life gives a clear biblical approach to practical personal finances, wealth generation, and the financing of the Great Commission in our day. When you read through the pages of this book, your mind will become renewed by the Word of God and you will start thinking more like God, who owns the cattle on a thousand hills. This book is the most complete work on this subject that I have read.

I really liked Brian's first book on finances, *Prosperity with a Purpose*. I found it both refreshing and revelatory. But *A Practical Path to a Prosperous Life* is a much better book because it gives the reader practical steps to experience God's prosperity and building wealth to finance the kingdom of God in our day. This book, like the first, is down to earth as Brian allows us to peer into the window of his own life as he gives his own personal stories of how this revelation has worked out practically for him.

I completely agree with my friend Rob Holman who says: "I believe there is a very strong anointing on this book that will powerfully impact thousands of people around the world! The three-part breakdown is perfect. The scope and sequence is wonderful, and the book is easy to understand with personal illustrations woven throughout."

Get ready to highlight large portions of this book so you can go back over it again and again as you develop a prosperous soul and experience the joy of seeing firsthand the kingdom of God advance through your faith and obedience in the financial realm. Thank you, Brian, for this major contribution to the church of the 21st Century!

Larry Kreider
DOVE International
International Director

Introduction

In the fall of 1997, I was taking some time to pray and seek the Lord. While I had my eyes closed worshiping the Lord, I saw a mental picture of a field of young corn stalks, like those I have seen many times in the early part of the summer in rural Pennsylvania where my family lives. The corn stalks were about eighteen inches high with very healthy, lush green stalks in neat rows with no weeds. The soil was dark and moist but not muddy. It was full of lumps like it had just been freshly tilled. As I watched the field, I noticed there was a slight rustling among the corn stalks; the leaves were gently shaking because a light, refreshing rain was falling on this fertile field.

I felt the Lord speak to me, "Teach my people to prosper, teach my people to prosper, teach my people to prosper, teach my people to prosper." I realized this was a commissioning by the Lord to teach a biblically based message of God's abundant provision. My first book *Prosperity with a Purpose* was written in response to this commissioning. That book seemed to help many people and give them a desire to learn more. I am a very practical person, so this book takes a step by step approach to systematically teach the practical things from God's word to help us to experience God's abundance and consequently fulfill his destiny for our lives.

Years ago there was teaching that emerged about God's desire to prosper Christians financially. At the core of this teaching was a revelation of God's nature that was biblical and accurate.

As the teaching was repeated, however, it became distorted and taken to extremes. This "whisper down the lane" perversion of the original biblical revelation caused the prosperity message to become tainted and subsequently dismissed by many. This is not the first time in church history a truth was restored to the church and taken to an extreme. C. Peter Wagner discusses this in his book *Churchquake!*

> Going to extremes while reemphasizing a half-forgotten Christian truth is not unusual. Early Calvinists went to extremes with the sovereignty of God, arguing for double predestination, which threatened to develop into Christian dualism. Early faith healers went to extremes such as choosing not to take medicine or go to a doctor. Early holiness advocates went to extremes and taught complete eradication theology. In all these streams, later generations invariably gravitated to a more moderate and more biblical position. When all is said and done, we are now grateful for more emphasis than there used to be on God's sovereignty, on praying for the sick and on personal holiness.[1]

We are looking for that moderate and biblical position described by C. Peter Wagner. I believe God wants to prophetically re-release the message of biblical prosperity to the church community. Bill Johnson speaks of this same need to focus on the truth of God's Word instead of the mistaken application of man. Johnson writes in his book *When Heaven Invades Earth*:

The abuses of a few in the area of prosperity does not excuse the abandonment of the promises of God to provide abundantly for his children. It is his good pleasure to do so. Because there is complete and perfect provision in heaven there must be the same here.

My dream is to help identify and eradicate the poverty mindset from the church. We must be set free to prosper. There are many prophetic scriptures that speak of a great increase of wealth into the kingdom of God in the last days. I am convinced we will need it all to accomplish his will for our lives.

Part I

Teach Me
to Prosper

CHAPTER 1

Isn't It More Spiritual to be Poor?

With tears in his eyes the veteran missionary looked at me. He had gathered his children and grandchildren around him at the front of the church building. I had just finished teaching that God wanted to be the God of "more than enough." Generally as I proclaim the message of biblical prosperity, people respond and ask for prayer to be free from poverty. But I realized God was doing something different as this man approached me with his extended family gathered around him.

Here was a precious man of God and his wife who had spent much of their lives on the mission field. As they approached me, he gathered his sons and daughters and put his arms around them. He wanted me to pray for his whole family. He shared that early in his life he had felt called to the mission field and told his wife and family that they would "always be poor" because they were called to be missionaries. He went on to share about their experiences of never having enough money. When they were on the mission field and when they were home, they never seemed to have enough, always barely scraping by. Now he saw the same lack in the lives of his children. He wanted me to pray for them and break the power over these words he had spoken over his family. He wanted his family to meet and know God as El Shaddai, the God of more than enough.

Knowing the power of our own will and words, I asked him to pray first and cancel his words of financial lack over himself and his family. He stood in his place of God-given leadership authority over his family and prayed. Then I followed in a prayer of financial blessing for the family as God met them in a beautiful time of prayer and restoration. The whole family left with a burden lifted anticipating God's abundant financial blessing. Who said missionaries should be poor anyway?

Voluntary poverty

One of the fun things I do when I am training leaders is to help them identify and develop their spiritual gifts. It is always such a pleasure to help people discover how God made them and gave them special grace in specific areas. This almost always helps them to find fulfillment and effectiveness in what God has called them to do. It is in taking a closer look at one of the spiritual gifts that we discover why some are confused and think it is more godly or spiritual to be poor.

In studying spiritual gifts we find a gift called voluntary poverty.[1] Voluntary poverty is defined as choosing to live below a normal standard of living to minister to a people group or an individual. It works many times alongside of the gift of missionary. Church history is full of stories of people who operated in this gift such as George Muller and John Wesley.

Could it be that some Christians see this gift in well-known missionaries and church leaders (past and present) and hear their powerful, inspirational testimonies; yet they make the mistake of thinking this is now the standard for everyone rather than a special grace that is given only to some? It seems that many times Christians who live in financial lack hold as their heroes of the faith some of these spiritual giants who had the gift of voluntary poverty, not realizing they themselves do not have the same grace. This could be the cause of some Christians not experiencing God's abundance in the area of finances.

In his book *Find Your Promised Land*[2], Korean businessman Israel Kim targets this same incorrect thinking.

> One of the lies taught about resources is that holy people should be poor. This concept of poverty and piety was developed during the Dark Ages by monastic orders of Catholic monks who were reacting to the audacious wealth, greed and corruption of the Roman Church. In those circumstances it may have seemed right, but in truth it is a curse that has kept many talented and anointed people from fulfilling their God-given destiny. They see how hard it is to simply survive and decide that living in poverty is no way to exist. The idea that poverty is a sign of humility and devotion to the Lord is simply false. If it were true the wretched poor within the "10–40 Window" would have no need for evangelization.

Many Christians say God is good, but because they have always struggled financially, they have developed a mindset that

God is stingy and is holding back blessings. There are two sides of this coin. We must be convinced that poverty and lack is a curse, and we must be convinced that God is a loving, abundant provider.

Poverty is a curse

It is important that we realize from reading the Bible that God considers poverty to be a curse. We find this to be true when we look at Job's story. God was blessing him with health and abundance; however, it was when Satan intervened that God's blessings were interrupted. Let's read it.

> "Does Job fear God for nothing?" Satan replied.
> "Have you not put a hedge around him and his house-
> hold and everything he has? You have blessed the work
> of his hands, so that his flocks and herds are spread
> throughout the land" (Job 1:9–10).

When Job was under attack from the devil he encountered poverty, sickness and calamity. A friend of mine is fond of saying that if you are not convinced that poverty is a curse, you should go on a trip to the poorest sections of India to see what it does to people. He notes that you will also be convinced of the close association of religion, poverty, sickness and death. All of these are included in the list of curses in Deuteronomy 28:15–68 for disobedience to God.

The first car that I ever owned had a problem with the trans-mission, and it would leave a puddle of fluid under my car when it sat in the same location for any length of time. I got into the habit of always looking under my car to check for a leak before

I drove it away. Sometimes the leak would be bad enough that it would leave a trail of fluid as I was driving away. Consequently, I developed the habit of always looking in my rear view mirror as I drove away to see if I was leaving a trail of fluid on the road. For many years I maintained this habit and expected something to be wrong with my vehicles even though they were mechanically sound and did not leak any fluids.

Was I really supposed to live like this? As I pondered it, I concluded that this was an expression of the spirit of poverty that had attached itself to me. I asked the Lord to help me break free of it. It took some time, but I can say that I am free from it today. I now enjoy driving the vehicles God has given us without the nagging fear that something is wrong mechanically or will go wrong with them.

God is a loving, abundant provider

I believe we must be totally convinced that God is an abundant provider—not just sometimes when he is in a good mood—but that his nature is to provide "more than enough." It is how he does things. Can you imagine standing there when Jesus turned the water into wine? The scripture says in the book of John that six stone water jars used for ceremonial washing, each holding from twenty to thirty gallons, were filled to the brim. Filled to the brim? By my calculation that would be 160 gallons of wine. We do not know how many guests were at the wedding, but that is a lot of wine. Abundance is part of his nature. He fed the five thousand men (not to mention women and children) and there were baskets of food left over.

Is our picture of Jesus really correct? Do we realize how Jesus lived? He was well taken care of by his Father. Jesus and his party were accused of living in celebration and luxury. Maybe it was true. Why was he welcome at parties with the gluttons and drunkards? This would have been the wealthy people of the community. Maybe they invited him because they were hoping he would turn more water into wine? I don't know.

Jesus was not destitute and poor. He was born in a manger because the inn was full. It was a symbolic act because he was the Lamb of God. His earthly father (Joseph) was a businessman going to pay taxes along with everyone else. Later, the wise men came to visit him in a house.

> On coming to the house, they saw the child with his mother Mary, and they bowed down and worshiped him. Then they opened their treasures and presented him with gifts of gold and of incense and of myrrh (Matthew 2:11).

Jesus himself was either self-employed or working in his father's business until age thirty. He was not homeless and poor. If it is more spiritual to be poor as some Christians think, then we would have to say that Jesus was not very spiritual!

Jesus took time to meet the needs of both wealthy men and poor beggars. However, when he called his disciples he spoke only to men who were successful, working businessmen. We find out at his crucifixion that Jesus wore clothing that was valuable. It was valuable enough that hardened soldiers did not want to destroy it. People followed Jesus because he had authority and knew where he was going. He had wealthy women traveling with his party. In fact, Luke indicates that the wife of the manager of Herod's household was traveling with Jesus and financially supporting him.

> After this, Jesus traveled about from one town and village to another, proclaiming the good news of the kingdom of God. The Twelve were with him, and also some women who had been cured of evil spirits and diseases: Mary (called Magdalene) from whom seven demons had come out; Joanna the wife of Cuza, the manager of Herod's household; Susanna; and many others. These women were helping to support them out of their own means (Luke 8:1–3).

Do you think that Joanna slept in the dirt? I do not know, but I doubt it. She was married to Herod's treasurer. I am inclined to think about what happens when we go to the mountains for a weekend with friends. When it is just the guys for the weekend, it is okay to rough it a little and just take the bare essentials. But when our wives accompany us, the environment tends to be a little more comfortable.

Jesus had a treasurer named Judas who carried a money box. I suppose we could say that the money box was empty, but do you really think Jesus would have had someone carry an empty money box around? I would be surprised if this was true. As stated previously, many Christians will say God is good, but because they have always struggled financially, they eventually can develop a mindset that God is stingy and holding back blessing, when just the opposite is true.

Without realizing it, we can communicate this stingy view of God to those around us. For years my wife and I were involved in training youth leaders to lead youth groups. Food and snacks for ravenous teens are a big part of youth ministry. As we trained youth leaders, one of the practical things we encouraged them to do in this area was to buy good quality, name brand soda and snack food to give to the kids. Why did we do this? Youth leaders are presenting a picture of the nature of God to the teens at a very impressionable age. Do we really want to demonstrate to them that God is a cheapskate who provides cheap stuff for his kids? No, we want them to see that God is a loving abundant provider.

God loves the whole world, but he has an agreement with those of us who are Christians. Let me explain by talking about the owner of our local professional sports team. The owner has a general relationship with the fans and invites them to come to the games and enjoy them. He wants them to come, and he does his best to put a winning team on the field for them to enjoy. If some fans get disappointed and angry, they can stop coming to the games and it is no big deal.

However, the owner of the team has a written contract with his players and coaches. There are specific commitments and expectations for both sides. They are legally bound to this commitment. In the same way, God has made an agreement with Christians through his word to provide abundantly for more than just their needs. Though we know he loves the whole world, he has a contract with those who have taken his offer and signed on to his team.

God delights in the prosperity of his servants

What does it mean when the scripture says he delights in the well-being (sometimes translated prosperity) of his servant?

> May those who delight in my vindication shout for joy and gladness; may they always say, "The Lord be exalted, who delights in the well-being of his servant" (Psalm 35:27).

It means it makes him happy to bless you, financially and otherwise! God wants to give you the desires of your heart. Let me qualify that by saying that as you get closer to him the desires of your heart are the same as the desires of his heart and your plans are his plans. He wants to give them to you:

> May he give you the desire of your heart and make all your plans succeed (Psalm 20:4).

In the next chapter we will explore the idea that it takes money to do things for God. If our heart's desire is to follow his will for our lives, we will find our desires in alignment with his desires.

NOTES

1   C. Peter Wagner, *Finding Your Spiritual Gifts* (California: Gospel Light, 2005).
2   Israel Kim, *Find Your Promised Land: Getting Through Your Wilderness* (Pennsylvania: Destiny Image Publishers, 2009).

Small Group Study Questions

1. How is voluntary poverty different than a spirit of poverty?

2. How do we know that poverty is a curse?

3. What did Jesus demonstrate by turning the water into wine?

4. What examples of a "stingy God" have been presented to you?

5. Explain what abundance means to you.

CHAPTER 2

It Takes Money to Do Things for God

I have a friend whose sister teaches a third-grade class. The following is a paragraph from one of her students' essays about money.

> I am thankful for all the money we have, all the one, two, five, ten, twenty, fifty, and one hundred dollar bills. And also, all the cents and coins, all the pennies, nickels, dimes, quarters, half dollars and one-hundred cent coins, and also all the kinds of money around the world, also all the checks and credit cards. Also all the people that invented money and coins. If the new one-thousand dollar bill comes, I will be thankful for it, also for gold money, also rings that are worth money.

This child might have a healthier attitude toward money than a lot of Christian adults. If we could just be honest, we would acknowledge that it takes money to do things for God. I used to be fond of giving a disclaimer when someone was fundraising for a project. I sometimes responded by saying that if I had a thousand dollars, I would give it. It sounded really spiritual and made me feel good about myself, but the honest truth was that I did not have the money to give. Proverbs 25:14 talks about one who defrauds others by "boasting of gifts not given." I have since stopped saying those words. Instead, I focus on trying to have funds available to give when needed.

C. Thomas Anderson is the founder and senior pastor of the Living Word Bible Church in Mesa, Arizona. He tells the story of a young man from his church who chose not to attend a wealth seminar.

> "With a tone of superiority in his voice, he explained that he had not been to any of the sessions, because he was not interested in money. That wasn't where God was leading him. Exactly twenty-four hours later he returned to the church. With tears in his eyes, he asked if the church could help by giving some money to his neighbor. A fire had destroyed everything she had owned, and she was left destitute with several children to care for. Suddenly money mattered. If this young man had seen the importance of money in ministry somewhat earlier in his life, he might have been in a better position to minister to his neighbor without having to ask others who did care about money."[1]

We cannot separate money and ministry. Most of us have heard and love the story of the Good Samaritan. We would all like to be the Good Samaritan that Jesus described. Let's read carefully the story:

> In reply Jesus said: "A man was going down from Jerusalem to Jericho, when he fell into the hands of robbers. They stripped him of his clothes, beat him and went away, leaving him half dead. A priest happened to be going down the same road, and when he saw the man, he passed by on the other side. So too, a Levite, when he came to the place and saw him, passed by on the other side. But a Samaritan, as he traveled, came where the man was; and when he saw him, he took pity on him. He went to him and bandaged his wounds, pouring on oil and wine. Then he put the man on his own donkey, took him to an inn and took care of him. The next day he took out two silver coins and gave them to the innkeeper. 'Look after him,' he said, 'and when I return, I will reimburse you for any extra expense you may have'" (Luke 10:30–35).

A study of the money of this time period reveals that the two coins the Good Samaritan gave to the innkeeper were enough to pay for keeping him two months at the inn.[2] Think about how much it would cost us today to keep someone at a hotel for two months with food costs. It would cost thousands of dollars.

The story of the Good Samaritan is the story of a man who had significant enough net worth (we will talk more about net worth later in Chapter 13) to take care of the robbery victim for two months. And it gets better, the Good Samaritan then continued on his journey while this man was cared for by someone he paid to do it. Because he had sufficient resources, he met this person's need, but wasn't distracted from the primary purpose of his trip. How many of us want to be the Good Samaritan? I know I do.

I find the Good Samaritan model attractive because I desire to multiply my efforts in expanding the kingdom of God. If I have the resources to pay or support others in ministry like the Good Samaritan did, it means that my efforts are multiplied. I can accomplish more than just what I do with my personal time and energy. I believe all of us were created with a desire to be productive.

From a mathematical perspective, we could compare how I spend my time as addition. It is time spent, and hopefully, well spent. However, when I can support or resource others concurrently this is more like multiplication. It seems like I am accomplishing more, which makes me feel more productive.

Generally speaking, business people have learned to get a good return on their money. They expect it to be productive. However, because of a dualistic mentality, sometimes Christians see pastors and missionaries as spiritual and business people as not spiritual. Business people are sometimes seen as having strings attached to their money because they will not give to a project unless they see a significant return. This is because they have become accustomed to their money accomplishing things; not even leaving money in the bank if it is not earning sufficient interest. They expect money to get something of value in return, and this is a perspective that benefits us all.

Financial independence

Permit me to introduce a term that many Christians consider to be a selfish, secular term—financial independence. Let's redefine "financial independence" as having the resources on hand that will be needed to obey God's voice. Too many times we have dismissed or not taken seriously the visions and ideas God has given to us because we do not see a way for them to be financed. Our excuse for not obeying God is a paltry, "That would be great, but we can't afford it." It is essential that we permanently delete the words "we can't afford it" from our vocabulary. These words should be replaced with a positive petition, expecting God's provision, by asking instead, "How is God going to provide?"

When God asked Noah to build the ark, he was at a place in his life with sufficient resources to obey. He was financially independent. There are no scriptures indicating Noah awakened one day, and the ark was miraculously finished. There is no record of ravens flying in with pre-cut gopher logs to be fitted into place. The ark was built with manual labor over a period of years. Actually, it seems like Noah did not work on the ark much himself because he was busy preaching. So either his family or hired laborers constructed the ark.

It took significant financial resources for Noah to obey God. Could it be that God wants to provide for us in a similar way? I believe he desires that we have the resources on hand to accomplish his purposes as he reveals them to us.

A similar example from the New Testament is that of Joseph from Arimathea. He was a rich man, a member of the Sanhedrin—who was a disciple of Jesus. Joseph was ready and available when called upon to take Jesus' body and give it an appropriate burial in a rich man's tomb that had never been used before. This was significant because in Bible times, tombs were used multiple times. His availability through his financial resources played an important symbolic role in the death and resurrection of Jesus and the unfolding of the kingdom of God.

More biblical examples

In 2 Kings, we find Elisha had a wealthy woman who took care of him so he could be effective in his prophetic ministry.

> One day Elisha went to Shunem. And a well-to-do woman was there, who urged him to stay for a meal. So whenever he came by, he stopped there to eat. She said to her husband, "I know that this man who often comes our way is a holy man of God. Let's make a small room on the roof and put in it a bed and a table, a chair and a lamp for him. Then he can stay there whenever he comes to us" (2 Kings 4:8–11).

How could this woman and her husband add a room on to their house for the prophet? Simply stated, they had the financial means to do so. This arrangement was a blessing to Elisha and also to the well-to-do woman as she later had a son who was raised from the dead by the prophet.

I doubt if you ever heard of Publius of Malta. I never heard of a sermon or Bible study about Publius; however, he was a key in the gospel spreading throughout Malta. In Acts it states that Paul stayed at Publius' estate for three months after his ship wrecked on Malta.

There was an estate nearby that belonged to Publius, the chief official of the island. He welcomed us to his home and for three days entertained us hospitably. His father was sick in bed, suffering from fever and dysentery. Paul went in to see him and, after prayer, placed his hands on him and healed him. When this had happened, the rest of the sick on the island came and were cured. They honored us in many ways and when we were ready to sail, they furnished us with the supplies we needed. After three months we put out to sea in a ship that had wintered in the island (Acts 28:7–11).

Maybe we should read that again? This passage clearly states that, after Publius' father was healed, all the sick on the island came and were healed. This was a full-blown healing revival. Since we know Paul's evangelism methods from other scriptures in Acts, we would have to assume that he followed these signs and wonders with the preaching of the word. Although the Bible does not say specifically, we know from historical accounts that many became Christians as a result of this three-month stay in Malta. Christians on Malta still celebrate the events of Paul's "accidental" visit to Malta.

How about the Ethiopian eunuch? He was an important official in charge of all the treasury of Candace, Queen of the Ethiopians. The Lord supernaturally directed Philip to leave the powerful revival in Samaria to meet this one man. God saw it as important to see this wealthy government official come to salvation. Let's read the account from Acts chapter eight.

Now an angel of the Lord said to Philip, "Go south to the road—the desert road—that goes down from Jerusalem to Gaza." So he started out, and on his way he met an Ethiopian eunuch, an important official in charge of all the treasury of Candace, queen of the Ethiopians. This man had gone to Jerusalem to worship, and on his way home was sitting in his chariot reading the book of Isaiah the prophet. The Spirit told Philip, "Go to that chariot and stay near it." Then Philip ran up to the chariot and heard the man reading Isaiah the prophet. "Do you understand what you are reading?" Philip asked. "How can I," he said, "unless someone explains it to me?" So he invited Philip to come up and sit with him (Acts 8:26–31).

This man was obviously an important government official, as described here, with great wealth entrusted to him and almost certainly a man of significant wealth himself to hold this position. We would assume this because of the position he held and because no government official would put someone in charge of a state treasury unless they had experience in managing their own personal money.

As we read on, we find that the Ethiopian eunuch was converted and baptized and that Philip was immediately translated from his presence. It is thought by church historians that Philip was the first to take the gospel to North Africa. Clearly in the Bible, God used people of means to accomplish his purposes.

Money must be your friend

God will not ask us to complete the Great Commission without money. This is very important. Jesus himself used the example of someone needing to count the cost of building a house before starting to build it. No responsible person would start building a house or start a business without carefully assessing beforehand what it will cost. It will take money to do what we are called to do on the earth, and the good news is God desires to give it to us.

Jesus ministered to wealthy individuals and to poor beggars. There is a rut on either side of the road—materialism and greed on one side and poverty and lack on the other side. Biblical prosperity as described in this book is the middle path of abundant provision to complete His purposes for our lives.

Many people in the church today live in an unhealthy fear of materialism. It is a fear that if God blesses us financially, it will somehow ruin us and cause us to fall away from Him. I used to think that a million dollars would taint and corrupt a person, but now I believe a million dollars will not corrupt you; it will only amplify what already is in your heart. If there is selfish ambition and pride in your heart, it will be amplified. If there is love and generosity in your heart, it will be amplified.

Many people mistakenly think of Solomon as an example of someone in the Bible who had great wealth and it caused him to trust God less. But the scriptures indicate Solomon was led into sin by disobedience related to his relationships; it was not necessarily related to his wealth. Nehemiah said:

Was it not because of marriages like these that Solomon king of Israel sinned? Among the many nations there was no king like him. He was loved by his God, and God made him king over all Israel, but even he was led into sin by foreign women (Nehemiah 13:26).

There were many great men and women of the Bible who experienced abundance and continued steadfast in their love for the Father.

The prosperity that comes from God comes without trouble, heartache and grief. A lot of us in the Western world, when we think of wealth, think of the lifestyles of the rich and famous people featured in gossip magazines. They are constantly divorcing and living a life of physical and emotional crisis and distress. Broken relationships, addictions, controversy and legal disputes seem to follow them wherever they go. Who would want to live like that?

However, it appears that the path of God's blessings is different. Let's examine a few more scriptures.

Whoever trusts in his riches will fall, but the righteous will thrive like a green leaf. The house of the righteous contains great treasure, but the income of the wicked brings them trouble (Proverbs 11:28; 15:6).

For the love of money is a root of all kinds of evil. Some people, eager for money, have wandered from the faith and pierced themselves with many griefs (1 Timothy 6:10).

Trouble, heartache and grief are not God's will for us. No... there is a path in God that avoids trusting in riches but allows for us to thrive like a green leaf. It is a path of financial blessing, abundance, joy, peace and fulfillment. This is the path that we want to find.

Russell Conwell was a Baptist minister during the early 1900's. He is famous as the founder of Temple University and Gordon-Conwell seminary still bears his name. Listen to Russell Conwell's thoughts on money and how it is used:

> Money is power, and you ought to be reasonably ambitious to have it. You ought because you can do more good with it than you could without it. Money printed your Bible, money builds your churches, money sends your missionaries, and money pays your preachers, and you would not have many of them, either, if you did not pay them.[3]

In conclusion, I have to say that it does take money to accomplish things for God. This helps me to raise my faith to expect God to supply money for what we are called to do. At the time of this writing, there is a major crisis in one of the nations of Africa where Christians are being persecuted and sold into slavery. In response, Western Christians are donating the finances to literally purchase the freedom of their brothers and sisters by buying them out of slavery. How could this ever happen without generous Christians with abundant financial reserves? It is difficult to avoid the idea that God wants his people to have an interest in money.

NOTES

1 Dr. C. Thomas Anderson, *Becoming a Millionaire God's Way* (New York: Hachette Book Group, 2006), 19.
2 *New International Version Study Bible Notes* (Michigan: Zondervan, 1985).
3 Russell Conwell, *Acres of Diamonds* (Pennsylvania: Temple University, 2012).

Small Group Study Questions

1. What would have happened if the Good Samaritan said, "I can't afford to help this man"?

2. What is one way to multiply the use of our time and finances?

3. What did you learn about Paul's visit to Malta?

4. Give some examples of wealthy people that God used in the Bible.

5. How do we know it takes money to do things for God?

CHAPTER 3

To Prosper Is a Good and Godly Desire

When my son was learning to play the trumpet, we needed to purchase one for him. If we bought the trumpet outright and paid for it in full, it would cost four-hundred dollars. However, if we did not have the four-hundred dollars and used the twenty dollars per-month-payment plan the music store offered us, we would end up paying six-hundred dollars for the trumpet. The question is, "Do we want to pay four hundred dollars or six hundred dollars for the same trumpet?" Four hundred of course! This is an amazing truth to grasp. When you have money you can live on less! This leaves more money for what we really want to do with it—like give and be a blessing! We have to crossover from living in lack to experiencing God's abundance; it will allow us to accomplish more.

Desire proceeds change

By now I hope that you are developing a healthy dissatisfaction with your level of income and your ability to finance God's kingdom at the level you would like. Dissatisfaction with the status quo is a very helpful first step to bring about change because it will generate desire and passion, which in turn will cause us to focus on solutions, such as those offered in this book.

The scriptures teach us in Timothy that godliness with contentment is great gain. I believe this means we should not complain about the place God has us in life. However, contentment does not mean we should pick up the paralyzing animistic belief of fatalism; the idea that our state in life is fixed and should not be improved. We should desire to advance and improve our life and the lives of people around us. It is a good and godly desire to prosper. It is good for you. It is good for your family. It is good for your neighborhood. It is good for the kingdom.

It is often said the definition of insanity is to repeat the same actions over and over again and expect to see different results. I hope you are dissatisfied enough to allow the Holy Spirit to show you some radical truth in the Bible that you have not seen before. Are you passionate enough to break out of some of your current patterns of thinking? Is your desire for change strong enough to stir you to take some new actions? I hope you are dissatisfied enough to apply the principles of this book. As you will find out shortly, it was a desire for more of God's provision that prompted me to search for and discover these principles.

What is the spirit of poverty?

I previously mentioned the spirit of poverty. I realize that not everyone is familiar with this terminology. Let me give some explanation. I call it a "spirit" and it is demonic, but it usually appears more as a pattern of thinking that is ingrained into our thinking, like a rut or groove from which we cannot escape. What is it and how can we identify it? Let's consider what Darrow Miller, in his book *Discipling Nations*, talks about concerning patterns of thinking that define the existence of peoples around the world.

> So why are people poor and hungry? Except for catastrophic events such as war, drought or flood, physical poverty does not "just happen." It is the logical result of the way people look at themselves and the world, the stories they tell to make sense of their world. Physical poverty is rooted in a mindset of poverty, a set of ideas held corporately that produce certain behaviors. These behaviors can be institutionalized into the laws and structures of society. The consequences of these laws and behaviors are poverty. In the West, we used to call it pauperism. While the word has been abandoned as old fashioned, the concept, poverty of mind, endures. Those with a poverty mind see the world through the glasses of poverty. They say or their actions say for them, "I am poor. I will always be poor, and there is nothing I can do about it."[1]

Rick Joyner, in his book *Overcoming the Spirit of Poverty*[2] takes this definition a step further. He states, "the spirit of poverty is a stronghold established for the purpose of keeping us from walking in the fullness of the victory gained for us at the cross, or the blessings of our inheritance in Christ."[2] The accuracy and truth of this definition resonated inside of me as I read it.

The spirit of poverty is a specific and strategic obstacle from the enemy to keep the church of Jesus Christ from growing and prospering. Is it more spiritual to be poor? I used to think it was, but the Lord has convinced me otherwise. I discovered that it does not take much faith to be poor. It seems to happen automatically. In fact, I started to wonder, "Is it really selfish and lazy for us to settle for just barely enough finances to meet our needs?" Especially when we have the capability to raise our faith and believe for much more in order to see the kingdom of God advance.

We need natural riches

I believe the devil is not as concerned about the church having spiritual riches (love, joy, peace and so forth) as long as he can hinder the church from receiving the natural riches needed to export the spiritual riches. The spirit of poverty must be rooted out of the church so that natural riches can be provided for us to complete our task of fulfilling the Great Commission. We have to move away from a dualistic mindset that says spiritual riches are good and natural riches are bad. Money is more than merely a necessary evil. It is a vital tool God wants to put in our hands so we can succeed in what we are called to do. In fact, as we read Luke 16:10–11 we see that God expects us to handle both well.

> Whoever can be trusted with very little can also be trusted with much, and whoever is dishonest with very little will also be dishonest with much. So if you have not been trustworthy in handling worldly wealth, who will trust you with true riches?

We have a mission

God has asked his church to fulfill the Great Commission. Would God ask us to fulfill the Great Commission and not provide the resources that we need to complete the job? I do not believe he would. It is against his nature, as I understand it from the scriptures, to frustrate and tease us by asking us to complete a job and then not give us the tools to accomplish that task. Money is simply a tool the church needs to complete its job description. As we examine the scriptures, we will find good reason to expect the financial provision needed for us to complete the task assigned to us.

Could it be that we have more available to us in the area of financial provision than we have asked for? Listen to Paul's words as he is writing to the Christians at Ephesus: "I pray also that the eyes of your heart may be enlightened in order that you may know the hope to which he has called you, the riches of his glorious inheritance in the saints, and his incomparably great power for us who believe." Somehow the Ephesians were missing part of their inheritance. Paul was praying for their eyes to be opened to it.

Is it possible that we, like the Ephesians, have missed part of our inheritance in Christ? Has the progress of our mission been slowed because we haven't asked for the tools we need to complete it? Has the spirit of poverty blinded our eyes and kept us from even asking for the finances needed to do the job?

An embarrassing story

My wife and I have always supported missions as a regular part of our budget. This has been our lifestyle since the first year of our marriage. Even before we were married, as singles we supported missionaries because we had a desire to see the gospel go to the entire world.

Over the years, we have endeavored to find ways to increase our giving, and a few years ago I had a "great idea" of how we could accomplish it. My brainstorm was for our family to eat rice and beans for a whole month and give the balance of the money we would save on groceries to missionaries. We had visited South America a number of times on mission trips and enjoyed eating rice and beans as the main food staple while there. I thought it would be a great project for us to do as a family and would model a giving lifestyle for our children. It seemed like a profoundly spiritual idea to me.

When I shared this deeply spiritual idea with my wife, she gave me an incredulous look and replied, "You can eat rice and beans for a month, but I am not, and I am not going to try and get our children to do it." Quickly realizing that my great idea was not meeting my wife's approval, I remember piously thinking how unspiritual she was for not adopting my idea. As I look back on this embarrassing incident now, I would have made a good Pharisee that day.

It only hit me a couple of years later how much the spirit of poverty had affected my thinking. I literally wanted to take food away from my wife and children so that we could give a few extra dollars to missions. Just what was wrong with this idea? I discovered this to be a form of poverty thinking. Let me explain why.

I did not believe that God could supply more for us so that we could give more. In my thinking, we were limited to my paycheck. I looked at the income we had and saw that as a fixed ceiling rather than believing God for more money. So I wanted to take food from my children's mouths and give it to missions. What picture of God (the Father) does that give to my children? It shows them he is a stingy Father, who gives us just enough or barely enough to survive. As we will explore in this book, this is not a biblically accurate picture of God. I realized it was not right for me to show my children this tainted portrayal of God.

Thank God for my wife who could see this was not an appropriate course of action. Although it seemed so spiritual at the time, I should have been raising my faith to lift the ceiling and believe for more—lots more—not just a few dollars to give to missions. The truth is, I did not want to give five dollars more a month to missions. I want to give fifty or five-hundred dollars more a month. This revelation has helped us to increase our giving significantly.

To be clear, the Christian life is one of self-sacrifice and surrender to his lordship and our children need to see that modeled before anything else. How we spend our money is part of that and obedience to his direction is essential. If God is directing you to save some money out of your budget by sacrificing something, then do it wholeheartedly. However, maybe you want to pray about increasing your inflow so you can give significantly more.

The icy chill of church offerings

Many times whenever the topic of money or finances is mentioned in church settings, there seems to be an icy chill that spreads across the group. I wondered about this, because every time an offering was taken, I always felt like quickly exiting the building. Why did I feel this way? What was this uncomfortable feeling? Where did it come from? Was it from God or the devil?

I came to realize the icy chill was not from God. I recognize it now as an aspect of the spirit of poverty sent from hell to strip the church of one of the tools it needs—money and one of the methods for how the tool should be used—giving. If we closely examine the Bible, we find it communicates about natural riches as well as spiritual riches. What good is it to possess spiritual riches if we do not have the means and the natural riches to get them to the people who need them?

Changing our thinking by examining the truth

Would you agree with me that many of us need to change our thinking in the area of finances? But, how will our thinking change? It will be adjusted by comparing our thoughts to the truth of the Word of God. We should renew our minds to what the scriptures inform us about finances. Money is a wonderful tool that God wants to give us to accomplish the mission he has given us.

Listen to what John the apostle, a close associate of Jesus, wrote to his fellow believer Gauis, "Beloved, I pray that in all respects you may prosper and be in good health, just as your soul prospers." John's "all respects" included financial prosperity because the context of the letter was advising Gauis about properly helping and taking care of traveling ministers.

Just as the apostle Paul was praying for the Ephesian believers, John, another of the early apostles, was praying for all things to go well just as the soul of the believer is getting along well. The term soul has to do with the mind and will. It is the thinking part of us. Could the way we think and believe actually affect the results we see in our lives? Does a spirit of poverty cause us to have poverty thoughts that lock us into a lifestyle of lack? If so, we should resist it with every fiber of our beings!

To prosper is a good and godly desire

Desire is a good motivator. I hope this chapter is stimulating a desire to see your finances change. We must be set free to prosper. I assure you we will closely examine the scriptures in the upcoming chapters, but for now ponder these introductory ideas and meditate on them. Could there be something we have been missing? Could the spirit of poverty be wrapped around and strangling you like it once held me?

God help us to identify if the spirit of poverty has affected our lives. In order to break free from the spirit of poverty, we need to understand how to replace those thoughts with truth. We desperately need a revelation of God's abundance. We have to understand that he is the God of "more than enough."

NOTES

1   Darrow L. Miller, *Discipling Nations* (Washington: YWAM Publishing, 1998), 67.
2   Rick Joyner, *Overcoming the Spirit of Poverty* (North Carolina: MorningStar Publications, 1996), 4.

Small Group Study Questions

1. Explain the following statement: "When you have money you can live on less."

2. What are some symptoms to help us recognize the spirit of poverty in the church? In our personal lives?

3. How can poverty thoughts be related to the spirit of poverty affecting our lives?

4. How can the spirit of poverty affect the way we respond to offerings and other opportunities to give?

5. Read Darrow Miller's quote again and ask yourself how you might be able to identify with his thoughts.

Chapter 4

Meet the God of
More than Enough

Calvin's story

Calvin Chiew, from Washington, D.C. in the United States, had a desire to do more for God and for others around him. It was after he read my first book on finances that he started a business that has grown to employ others. In a recent conversation, he shared how blessed he is to provide jobs for others who have lost their jobs because of an economic recession in the United States. He was blessed to be a blessing just like Abraham had been. Here are his comments.

> For me, personally, the book *Prosperity with Purpose* couldn't come at a better time. It reclaimed the word *prosperity* from the lies and misconceptions in me. I'm a very driven person, probably due to my upbringing and family background. As a Christian, I always thought there is something wrong with me, that I shouldn't have this strong desire to succeed in life. I thought a Christian should be content and stay "low key." I have a poverty mindset.

The book showed me there is nothing "low-key" about the God we serve. There is nothing poor about our God. He is "The Almighty," "The Magnificent One" and "The Many-Breasted One." I started to think and reflect upon His abundance. Like a loving parent, he yearns to give good things to his children. In fact, He is the giver of all good things. I started to believe He is going to bless me. And He did.

In the parable of the talents, the first two servants know the master's heart and they prosper. The simple truth is, prosperity implies responsibilities. Therefore, there is no shame in seeking and asking God for prosperity or success as long as we are aligned with Him. Nehemiah prayed to God for success and asked King Artaxerxes for lumber, not only enough for the walls and gates of Jerusalem, but also for his own house.

I want to briefly review this same revelation of God that I laid out in *Prosperity With a Purpose*.[1] In the same way that Abraham passed this revelation on to his son Isaac and Isaac to his son Jacob and Jacob to his son Joseph, I want to pass it on to you.

Prosperity with a purpose

Many of us are familiar with the biblical names used to progressively describe part of God's character and attributes to the children of Israel. We have heard names like Jehovah Rophe (our healer) and Jehovah Nissi (our banner). Another one of the early revelations of God came with the Hebrew name El Shaddai. Abraham was the one who was first introduced to El Shaddai.

Before we see how God introduced himself to Abraham as El Shaddai, let's examine Abraham's first revelation of God. It is found in Genesis 12:1–3.

> The Lord had said to Abram, "Leave your country, your people and your father's household and go to the land I will show you. I will make you into a great nation and I will bless you; I will make your name great, and you will be a blessing. I will bless those who bless you, and whoever curses you I will curse; and all peoples on earth will be blessed through you."

Here in Abraham's original promise of God's blessing is found what I call prosperity with a purpose. This verse clearly states that God will bless Abraham, and Abraham will be a blessing to others. This is still what he is saying to us today, "I will bless you and make you a blessing." This general declaration of blessing becomes a whole lot more specific in Genesis 17:1–6 when God introduces himself to Abraham as El Shaddai.

> When Abram was ninety-nine years old, the Lord appeared to him and said, "I am God Almighty (El Shaddai); walk before me and be blameless. I will confirm my covenant between me and you and will greatly increase your numbers." Abram fell facedown, and God said to him, "As for me, this is my covenant with you: You will be the father of many nations. No longer will you be called Abram; your name will be Abraham, for I have made you a father of many na-tions. I will make you very fruitful; I will make nations of you, and kings will come from you. I will establish

my covenant as an everlasting covenant between me and you and your descendants after you for the generations to come, to be your God and the God of your descendants after you."

This term, "God Almighty" in verse one is the English translation of the term El Shaddai. Wherever we find the term "God Almighty," it is speaking of the revelation of God using the Hebrew name El Shaddai.

The God of more than enough

Who is El Shaddai? Here is my favorite definition and the one we will use…El Shaddai is the God of "more than enough." *Enough* is that which is required to meet our needs. *More than enough* is having extra left over to meet the needs of others. The revelation of El Shaddai brought with it a pronouncement of fruitfulness and prosperity. We read later in Genesis of God's promise coming to pass for Abraham, especially as his servant Laban reports of his great wealth.

> So he [Laban] said, "I am Abraham's servant. The Lord has blessed my master abundantly, and he has become wealthy. He has given him sheep and cattle, silver and gold, menservants and maidservants, and camels and donkeys. My master's wife Sarah has borne him a son in her old age, and he has given him everything he owns" (Genesis 24:34–36).

We find that not only was Abraham blessed, but he also passed the revelation of El Shaddai on to his children. God is the God of Abraham, Isaac and Jacob. In Genesis 25:21, we find Isaac praying for his barren wife Rebekah to get pregnant.

> Isaac prayed to the Lord on behalf of his wife, because she was barren. The Lord answered his prayer, and his wife Rebekah became pregnant.

We have no indication why Rebekah was barren, but Isaac knew his father had told him about a God who promised fruitfulness and blessing. His wife's barrenness did not seem to fit the picture his father had painted, so he prayed, and the Lord made his wife fruitful. He had a revelation of El Shaddai.

Prosperity for all areas of our lives

When speaking of prosperity, I am using it within the context of finances, but this is only to help us get a handle on God's desire to prosper us. In reality, God wants to prosper us and make us fruitful in every area of our lives. He wants to prosper us in our physical bodies, our relationships, our marriages, our families, our vocations and even our emotions.

Later in Genesis, we read the amazing story of Isaac prospering in Canaan during an extended season of drought.

> Now there was a famine in the land—besides the earlier famine of Abraham's time.... Isaac planted crops in that land and the same year reaped a hundredfold, because the Lord blessed him. The man became rich, and his wealth continued to grow until he became very wealthy. He had so many flocks and herds and servants that the Philistines envied him (Genesis 26:1, 12–13).

Isaac personally introduced his son Jacob to El Shaddai in Genesis 28:1–3. Let's read it.

> So Isaac called for Jacob and blessed him and com-
> manded him: "Do not marry a Canaanite woman. Go
> at once to Paddan Aram ... Take a wife for yourself
> there, from among the daughters of Laban.... May
> God Almighty bless you and make you fruitful and
> increase your numbers until you become a community
> of peoples."

Here we see El Shaddai specifically mentioned in the same breath with "fruitfulness and increase" as Isaac seeks to pass on this revelation of God to his son. I am not sure why—perhaps Jacob did not quite understand what his father was saying—but he ended up getting a personal introduction to El Shaddai, complete with a name change just like his grandfather in Genesis 35:9–12.

> After Jacob returned from Paddan Aram, God ap-
> peared to him again and blessed him. God said to him,
> "Your name is Jacob, but you will no longer be called
> Jacob; your name will be Israel." So he named him
> Israel. And God said to him, "I am God Almighty; be
> fruitful and increase in number. A nation and a com-
> munity of nations will come from you, and kings will
> come from your body. The land I gave to Abraham
> and Isaac I also give to you, and I will give this land
> to your descendants after you."

A prosperous soul

Joseph, one of Jacob's sons, was next in line to receive the revelation of God Almighty (El Shaddai). The God of Abraham, Isaac and Jacob was passed on to the next generation in Genesis 48:3–4.

> Jacob said to Joseph, "God Almighty appeared to me at Luz in the land of Canaan, and there he blessed me and said to me, 'I am going to make you fruitful and will increase your numbers. I will make you a community of peoples, and I will give this land as an everlasting possession to your descendants after you.'"

Joseph received the revelation. We find that Joseph had this sense of prosperity in his soul. He had it inside of him. Wherever he was, whatever the situation, no matter how difficult, he eventually prospered. He seemed to rise to the top like cream rises to the top of milk.

When he was sold into slavery, he prospered. When he was in Potiphar's household, he flourished. Even in prison, he thrived. As the one in charge of the Egyptian government's food supply program, he prospered. He was the steward of more than enough to help others in their time of need during the seven years of famine. Prosperity was in his heart. He knew God wanted to bless him and prosper him no matter what his present circumstances.

This is what we are looking for: prosperity flowing out of our hearts regardless of where we are in our current situation. If we have prosperity of heart, we will find a way to prosper, no matter what our circumstances or the opposition facing us. It will not matter the condition of our local economy or if we have a savings account or if we are a single parent, because our prosperous heart will cause us to prosper.

What about Jehovah Jireh?

If you have been around Christians for any length of time, you have probably heard someone in financial need boldly declare, "My God shall supply all your needs according to His riches in glory[3]." As you will soon find out, I have prayed this prayer many times for myself. Perhaps you have even sung a song with words referring to Jehovah Jireh, my provider.

The phrase "My God shall supply all of your needs" is a direct quote from Paul writing to the Christians in Philippi. The idea was originally introduced in an Old Testament story of Abraham and his son Isaac where God is called Jehovah Jireh. The term Jehovah Jireh is another one of the Hebrew names for God which means, "The Lord will provide."

If we read the whole story in Genesis, we find that Abraham was told to offer his son as a sacrifice to the Lord. In obedience, Abraham took his son to the place of sacrifice. But at the last moment, it was revealed that this was only a test, and Abraham's son Isaac should not be offered as a sacrifice. I am sure everyone breathed a collective sigh of relief, especially Isaac. This was good news; however, if Isaac was not the sacrifice, what was to be offered?

God met the need

The offering was provided in the form of a ram caught in a thicket. This miraculous situation was used as an opportunity to introduce the children of Israel (and us) to an aspect of God's nature. He is the God who makes provision for all of our needs.

This is the precise revelation I had of God in the area of finances for most of my Christian life. I believed, prayed and expected this many times—that God would provide all of my needs. I never considered I could ask for more, and to be honest, I felt more spiritual for not asking. If we defined El Shaddai as the "God of more than enough," Jehovah Jireh must then be the "God of enough."

Do you know what I discovered? God met our every need all of those years when we believed for his provision only. The problem was, there was never anything left over. We had our needs met, but just barely, with thirty-two cents remaining at the end of the month.

He is more than the God of enough

As I started to ponder the things I am discussing, this revelation of El Shaddai would not go away. I felt stirred in my heart to change the focus of my faith and expectation from Jehovah Jireh to El Shaddai. So I did. I prayed and asked the Lord for more than enough. The most amazing things began to happen. Literally within months our personal finances began to change. We began to have surpluses. We started to experience more than just having our needs met.

After a year I could not keep it to myself. I felt guilty for not telling people about what I had found in the scriptures and was experiencing in my personal life. I had to reveal God's truth and revelation of his provision to others. It was too good to keep to myself and my family. To be very clear, the only thing we changed was our faith and expectation of how God was going to supply. I did not get an extra job. No one took an offering for us. We changed what we were expecting and what we were praying and our finances began to change.

It eventually dawned on me that the more we live with an understanding of El Shaddai, the less we would need the revelation of Jehovah Jireh. I say this in the fear of the Lord, knowing that there will always be times when I will need Jehovah Jireh to provide supernatural provision. But I definitely changed my pattern of thinking and my expectation of what God wants to do in the area of finances. When I started to grasp the concept of more than enough, I found it everywhere I looked!

What do I do with the surplus?

All of my life I had been thinking in terms of just getting what I needed. For example, in the area where we live it is common to cover the flower beds around the houses with bark mulch to keep the weeds from growing. When I purchased bark mulch to put on the flower beds at our house, I would carefully measure how many square feet of beds we had and figure how deep it should be covered and order just the right amount. My intention was to purchase just enough. I did not want any extra; because I was afraid it would go to waste. I almost always did not have enough to complete the task and had to make another trip to get more.

When I began to understand that my God was a God of more than enough, I started to order more mulch than I needed, asking God what he wanted me to do with the extra. Hmm…maybe my neighbor needs some?

Needs and joys

On a trip to the nation of Israel I found this principle alive in Jewish culture. Every Friday night the Sabbath celebration in a practicing Jewish home contains the giving of thanks to God for the bread and the wine after the meal. This practice is not what Christians know as the Lord's Supper. But by giving thanks for the bread, they are expressing appreciation for their basic needs of life being met. By giving thanks for the wine, they are expressing appreciation for the joys of life—the joys are the blessings of God that go beyond the meeting of their basic needs. Jews understand this very important concept about the nature of God.

Here is Frank Remley's story from Edmonton, Alberta, Canada:

> "The teaching on El Shaddai helped us to step out of the daily grind as a means of earning a living and to trust God to supply through a more entrepreneurial route. Prior to this, my income was largely based on the formula: "hours worked" equals "income received." We knew God had to have another way. As we learned more of God's heart to bless His people, we grew confident in His leading to step out of our comfort zone and into a new business—house building. We definitely have more financial risk, but we also have more opportunity to see God's hand of blessing.
>
> What can we say? He has been more than faithful! Our income in the first half year in this endeavor was more than double the previous half year's income. And not only did we experience the God of more than enough, but in our endeavor, we also experienced Jehovah Jireh, the God of miracles. The first two houses we built sold the same day, less than a week before Christmas, after only a couple of weeks on the market. God is good!"

In the next chapter we will take a closer look at how this revelation of "the God of more than enough" grew in my life as it can also grow in your life.

NOTES

1   Brian Sauder, *Prosperity with a Purpose* (Pennsylvania: House to House Publications, 2003)
2   Nathan Stone, *Definition of El Shaddai from Names of God* (Illinois: Moody Press), p.34
3. Philippians 4:19

Small Group Study Questions

1. Why do you think God used different names to describe himself to the children of Israel?

2. Give two examples of how God has met your needs in the past.

3. In the Jewish Sabbath celebration, what does the bread represent? What does the wine represent?

4. Abraham passed the blessing of God on to his family line. In the modern world, how can we see this happen?

5. When believing God for more than enough, there is often a surplus. What are your ideas to distribute the surplus?

Chapter 5

There's More

I already knew how to budget and some biblical principles about money. Still I constantly needed help from my church to pay for food or car repairs. After hearing the teaching of *Prosperity with a Purpose*, I stopped looking at the checkbook balance. I began instead to look to El Shaddai, "the God of more than enough" as my supply. Since then I have testified so many times about the many miracles in my finances that my friends got jealous. Now at their request, I am teaching others what the Bible says about money and our God—El Shaddai. And yes, lots of times, as God leads, I too give all that I have in my purse and the amount in there is increasing.

—Dorothy Carlson
Reading, Pennsylvania, United States

Dorothy's story is just one of many who discovered that God wants to be El Shaddai. About the same time I was discovering the revelation of El Shaddai, I had ordered a new Bible. I received the Bible, but it was not the correct size I had ordered. When I contacted the publisher, they instructed me to just send in the first page inside the cover and they would send me another Bible. As it turned out, the publisher sent two new Bibles by mistake. Now I had three study Bibles. All of a sudden I had more than enough Bibles! It seemed like the Holy Spirit was underlining this fresh revelation of God as the provider of more than enough. By the way, I did send the one Bible back, but with the publisher's permission, I gave the other to my wife. God blessed me, and I was able to be a blessing to my wife.

More than enough for my family

My wife and I have always had a dream to have a large family. However, many times when we shared our desire with friends, the response was always the same, even from some of our family members. How will you be able to afford so many children? We did not really have a good answer at the time. Usually we halfheartedly responded about God supplying somehow.

We just assumed it would take all that we have financially to raise our family. It even sounded rather spiritual, saying that we would put all that we had into our children. Sometimes, we continued by saying that we would not have natural riches, but that our children would be our riches.

As God was teaching us this new revelation of himself, one day my wife came to me and said we needed to stop believing and saying that it would take all we had financially to raise our family. She was right. We began to realize this was believing and expecting God to meet our needs but not believing that he would meet above and beyond our needs. Our faith and our words had to change if we wanted to see financial abundance. We specifically started to believe and say we would have all of our family's financial needs met and there would be finances left over for our family to support missionaries, give to others in need or to minister to those in our community.

God showed us we needed to change what we believed, what we said and what we expected. We now have five children, two in college, and are experiencing more than enough time and money for our family. We praise God because he is more than enough.

I have repeated these words "more than enough" so often my children learned them and looked for places where God was giving more than enough. We started to identify and expect to find this principle in multiple areas of our family life. I have more examples in the following chapters. Wait until you hear the story of the one hundred dollar bills!

A divine lifestyle

God's heart for abundant provision and blessing is at the core of the kingdom of God and its expansion. It is not an idea a preacher invented in order to collect a big offering. This is a scriptural teaching of provision. It is a divine lifestyle available to all believers.

I do realize there are different seasons including dry times and droughts, and we will examine these more thoroughly later. But, as we will see in the chapters to come, the scriptural pattern is one of more than enough. If we have faith to only meet our needs, then it is likely we will only have thirty-two cents left after we pay the monthly bills. It is important that we have faith for more than enough. If we have the faith and expectation of God's provision as more than enough, we will receive more than enough. I know that many Christians live their lives simply expecting God to only meet their needs. If this is you, I want to challenge you that there is more, much more.

What about financial miracles?

A minister friend of mine stated that people who have many testimonies of how God delivered them from repeated financial crisis are not the ones who we should pattern our financial lives after. Why? Because with all the miracles they have seen, they seem to still be in need of another miracle today to financially make it. In other words, although they have faith for financial miracles, they have not found faith to receive from God for long term abundant provision. They are still living (wandering) in the desert instead of entering into the Promised Land.

When the children of Israel were wandering in the wilderness, they received a daily miracle for their food called manna. It was fresh and new every day. It was miraculous provision. However, it could not be kept for the next day because any surplus would spoil. There was a complete dependency on God for provision every day. This seems to be similar to living by a revelation of Jehovah Jireh.

Should Christians live in the promised land today?

Manna was not God's long-term plan for provision. When God took them into the Promised Land, the daily manna stopped. It was no longer an option. In the Promised Land, the children of Israel were expected to live by the principle of sowing and reaping and seedtime and harvest. Let's look at the scripture where the transition happened. It is found in Joshua:

The day after the Passover, that very day, they ate some of the produce of the land: unleavened bread and roasted grain. The manna stopped the day after they ate this food from the land; there was no longer any manna for the Israelites, but that year they ate of the produce of Canaan (Joshua 5:11–12).

This was a different revelation of God's provision for the children of Israel. It included faith, but now they were also expected to farm the land, to sow and reap. They were expected to have an abundance because provisions were made to help the non-Israelites in their midst as well as bring the first fruits into the storehouse and make other offerings. There was also a whole group of people, the Levites, who were to be supported out of the abundance of the general population. In the desert, their sandals did not wear out for forty years, but in the Promised Land their sandals wore out and they had the resources for new sandals. This seems to be similar to living by the revelation of El Shaddai that was first introduced to Abraham.

The Promised Land was a concept indicating Israel's possession of a place with God in the earth where there was security from all external threats and internal calamity. It was a place of rest for the people of God to grow and prosper. If this was true for the children of Israel, then can we boldly ask ourselves what is God's will for Christians in the area of financial provision today? Is it God's will for Christians to live in the desert or is it God's will for Christians to live in the Promised Land?

God's blessing versus God's miracles

Without minimizing God's miracles, I now believe the more

we live in God's blessings, the less we will have to live by God's miracles. For example, the more we live in God's promise of divine health, the less we will need God's miracles of healing. Many churches teach that God will heal your body when you get sick. But how many teach divine health, believing that God will give you a divinely healthy life, free from sickness and disease? The more we walk in divine health, the less we will need physical healing.

We have already applied this same thought to the financial realm. The more we live in God's promise of divine prosperity, the less we will need God to do financial miracles in our lives. God's miracles rescue us in times of crisis; however, we can say that living in God's blessings keep crisis from coming.

When God intervenes and solves a crisis by a miracle, it is as if he is working for us. When God brings blessing into our lives in response to us obeying his Word or sowing seed, it is like he is working with us. Miracles are God overcoming the natural laws of the earth. Blessings are God working with the natural laws of the earth, like sowing and reaping, to bring his blessings into our lives. Both blessings and miracles are supernatural and come from God.

Living by God's miracles could leave you with a car that requires prayer for a miracle every time you need it to start. I can hear the groaning—too many of us have been there! The amazing thing is that God in his mercy will in some miraculous way help you get your car started. But unfortunately, you will still need another miracle to get it started the next day. Living in God's blessings can bring you a new car that will start every time you need it to start.

God's nature is seedtime and harvest

Miracles are usually just enough to get us through a crisis, but because God's blessings contain more than enough, the surplus can many times become someone else's miracle, meeting their needs. God's blessings are usually the fruit of something we have planted somewhere along the way. Fruits generally have the seeds in them to plant for the next crop. God's miracles are usually once and done. There is no seed in them. God's nature is seedtime and harvest; miracles are God's mercy.

Does it take more faith to believe for daily miracles or for a lifestyle of blessing, healing and prosperity? I think it takes more faith to live a lifestyle of blessing. God has provided miracles even when there was no faith. Do you remember the water from a rock and manna in the morning? These were miracles God did just to get the children of Israel to stop complaining. There was no great faith there! Could it require greater faith to live a lifestyle of blessing? The answer from my life experience is "yes."

Please keep in mind as I contrast El Shaddai and Jehovah Jireh, I am not talking about two separate gods. I am talking about two separate revelations of God's nature given to humanity with finite minds, to somehow gain an understanding of an infinite being. I am not creating new theology. I am introducing us to a divine aspect of our heavenly Father that some of us have not yet experienced. Appendix A has dozens of other scriptures in both the Old and New Testament that display God as the one who provides "more than enough."

As I was writing this book, God blessed us with more than enough again. Our local church has a sports team on which I participated. As I was changing clothes one day in the parking lot for a game, I took off my wedding band and must have inadvertently dropped the ring as I was putting my clothes into an athletic bag. I soon discovered my wedding band was missing. This was disappointing to both my wife and me. It was not a very expensive ring. It was more the idea that the ring represented the most important covenant in my life.

After a few months of hoping it would turn up somewhere, my wife and I went to a jewelry store to replace it. We found the prices of rings had increased almost tenfold since we had initially purchased the ring twenty-three years earlier. We were preparing to buy an inexpensive ring, when the jeweler remembered getting a return of an expensive ring. He found it and was able to size it to fit my finger. This attractive ring was worth three times what we would have spent for the least expensive ring there, but he gave it to us for the price of the least expensive ring.

What a blessing for God to prove his lavishness to us again and affirm our marriage covenant with a special blessing. God is good. I enjoy teaching this revelation of El Shaddai so much because it seems to help people to fulfill their destiny. Of all the things I teach as a Bible teacher, this area of biblical prosperity seems to help people the most in reaching their God-given dreams. Listen to the story of Merle and Cheree Shenk, missionaries in Cape Town, South Africa.

> Life in the mission field has been a journey of faith for us. After reading *Prosperity With A Purpose*, we really took a mental shift to believe that God could be the God of more than enough for us and our ministry. Many times we have seen God do amazing provisions. One story that stands out to me is the day our car broke down for the fourth time in one week, each time it was

something different. Our family was sitting beside the road, crying out to God, feeling ready to give up and leave South Africa. It was the week we were to launch our Bible School curriculum and it seemed as if the devil was pulling out all the stops. Two days later we were driving home a brand new, completely paid for new vehicle. Now we are learning to take offensive steps of faith with our finances in giving and growing the kingdom. This has been a mighty revelation that has changed our approach to daily living!

Small Group Study Questions

1. What are the reasons why testimonies of God's miraculous provision might actually keep us from experiencing his abundance?

2. How do we know it is God's will for Christians today to live in the Promised Land?

3. Give an example of how life was different for the children of Israel in the Promised Land than in the desert.

4. A good car that starts versus having one that you need to pray for a miracle in order to start it each morning is used as an example of God's blessings. Give another possible modern-day example.

5. Explain in your own words the phrase "God's nature is seed-time and harvest."

CHAPTER 6

Holy Spirit, Teach Me to Prosper

As I was getting this revelation of El Shaddai, I felt the Lord was prompting me to pray and ask the Holy Spirit to teach me to prosper. Knowing the scripture reveals that the Holy Spirit is our teacher, I decided to go for it. In prayer one day, I spoke these words, "Holy Spirit, teach me to prosper." I did not know what I was getting into, but I knew my thinking had to change.

Shortly after praying this prayer, I was in a Sunday morning church service and the speaker was teaching about some deep theological truth from the Bible. In the middle of his message, he stopped and asked this question, "How many people present know how many one hundred dollar bills there are in circulation for every one dollar bill?"

Most of the people were wondering what was going on and why he had departed from his topic. "Are there more one hundred dollar bills in circulation in United States currency or one dollar bills?" he repeated again. He paused for a few moments and then went on to give the answer: There are sixty one-hundred-dollar bills in circulation for every one-dollar bill. The speaker suggested perhaps Christians think in the wrong terms. Maybe we are thinking in terms of one dollar bills when we should be thinking in terms of hundred dollar bills.

My thinking was challenged

Most of the people in the congregation that day were wondering why the speaker couldn't stay on his topic, but not me. I had a clear sense that the speaker's digression from his sermon was specifically for me. Within two weeks, I was attending a leadership conference for pastors and listening to another speaker. This time the speaker was teaching on finances. Believe it or not, part of the way into his teaching he asked the question, "How many people here know how many one hundred dollar bills are in circulation for every one dollar bill?"

This got my attention. I knew God was speaking to me, but the question for me was, "Where are they? Where are the one hundred dollar bills, because I surely do not have any?" It was really clear that God was speaking to me. My thinking was being challenged. He wanted me to step out in faith and change my way of thinking. I was pondering this currency revelation God had shown me and trying to figure out how I could think in terms of hundreds instead of ones. The following is how the Holy Spirit directed me to change my actions. Remember, this is my real life story. It does not get any more practical than this.

God gives a practical plan

I realized that when I went to the bank, I would often withdraw more than one-hundred dollars in cash. I would take out $120 or

$150 or whatever was needed for the time. I felt the Holy Spirit prompting me to start asking for a one hundred dollar bill from the bank teller, whenever I withdrew more than one hundred dollars from the bank. If I withdrew more than $200, I asked for two one hundred dollar bills. The idea seemed kind of silly and a little bit embarrassing to me. Would God really tell me to do this? But, the impression would not go away, so I decided to obey.

It was hard at first. I felt really self-conscious and embarrassed asking the bank teller for the one hundred dollar bills. "I can do this," I kept telling myself. "God wants me to do this. He is teaching me." So from time to time, depending on my personal business, I would have a hundred dollar bill in my wallet. Eventually, I started to get a little more comfortable with it. This continued for a few months.

He is taking me seriously

One Sunday morning, I was sitting in our local church service with a one hundred dollar bill in my wallet. After the speaker shared his message that morning, it was announced there was going to be a special offering taken for him. I immediately stiffened because I knew in an instant what God wanted me to do. God was saying, "Okay, Brian, now you have a hundred dollar bill in your wallet, I want you to put that one hundred dollar bill in the offering." I admit it was a struggle. For some reason, it is much harder to depart with a hundred dollar bill than to write a check for the same amount. There is something about seeing it go. But I did it. It was an act of obedience, and it felt good.

God spoke to me immediately and said, "I will take you seriously in this venture if you take me seriously. I will bless you with hundreds if you are willing to give hundreds." You see, I was thinking in terms of receiving hundreds from God, and he was thinking of me giving hundreds to His work.

If you are considering praying this same prayer, "Holy Spirit, teach me to prosper," do so at your own risk. This lesson has been so real that I can honestly say without bragging that since that time, we have often given away one hundred dollar bills. We have been blessed. At the time of this writing, we are giving more money away and receiving more money than we ever have in our lives. By God's grace this principle continues to work in us and through us.

Do something different

I have found that if you desire to enter into something new in your relationship with God, you will have to relate to him differently than you have in the past. If you desire different results, your actions must be different. Unless your actions change, the results that follow will remain the same. But before your actions can change, your thoughts must change. God was prompting me through this thought-changing process.

The one-hundred-dollar-bill story is one practical example of how the Holy Spirit was teaching me to prosper by changing my thoughts and corresponding actions. The Holy Spirit began to show me that I had a "poverty mindset." The spirit of poverty had warped my thinking to the point that it had a poverty bent to it. My mind had to be changed and have the poverty bent ironed out of it. This next example was part of breaking out of the spirit of poverty and the beliefs that go with it.

The Christmas tree story

One year God blessed us with a magnificent Christmas tree for our home. The tree was on a special sale because the growers were phasing out this particular kind of tree. It was a huge tree, and fortunately we had a cathedral ceiling in our living room or it would not have fit in our home. It looked like a tree that cost a hundred dollars, but in actuality, it only cost us fourteen dollars.

The tree was so big we did not have enough Christmas decorations to cover it. We had to go out and buy more decorations. We decorated the tree and got ready to enjoy the Christmas season with our family. We were set for a great holiday season. There was only one problem. I discovered that when people came into our home to visit and saw the towering tree, they always commented about how big it was. However, this wasn't the problem. The problem was my reaction.

Their comments often were, "Wow, what a huge Christmas tree." When they said that, the spirit of poverty would rise up inside me, and I felt like I had to apologize for having such a big tree. I had a compulsion to tell them that I only paid fourteen dollars for the tree so they would not think I had paid a lot of money for it. So, out of my mouth would come the words, "Yes, it was on sale and we bought it for only fourteen dollars." I began to hate these words coming out of my mouth. It happened more than once. It was like an automatic response that I could not control. Something in me had to apologize for God's blessing. I did not like my response, and I began to think I needed some type of deliverance or breakthrough.

I could not help but notice the same thing in other areas of my life. If I was wearing a jacket that my wife bought at a secondhand shop for a few dollars and I received a compliment, immediately the response would come out of my mouth that it was used and we bought it for only a few dollars. I could not let people think that God had blessed me with something nice. I began to cry out to God for deliverance. The spirit of poverty says it is more spiritual to be poor or act like you are poor. It was obvious to me that God was teaching me this was not true.

Breaking the spirit of poverty

I started to pray for this spirit of poverty to be broken off of my life. Part of the answer was to realize I had to let people think that I had paid a hundred dollars for the tree. It was extremely difficult for me to do, but finally after someone else commented about our large tree, I was able to bite my lip, swallow the apology and say, "Yes, God blessed us with a big Christmas tree. God loves me and a big tree was an expression of his love for our family." Feeling freedom come over me, I knew I was making progress. The Holy Spirit was changing my beliefs, renewing my thoughts, and changing my actions all the while he was teaching me to prosper.

This does not mean we purchased a huge Christmas tree every year after this. Some years we did and some years we did not, but God used this experience to teach me to stop apologizing for His blessings. God was changing me in answer to my "teach-me-to-prosper" prayer. Ah! There is a better way. Somehow this seemed like a path that a good and loving God would provide for His children. The Holy Spirit was teaching me to prosper.

I guess by now you might realize what challenge I am giving to you. Would you be willing to pray the same risky prayer that

I did, "Holy Spirit, teach me to prosper?" Will you take God at his Word as we have studied it?

Did not strive to be prosperous

I want to caution you not to think about getting a second or third job and working twice as hard to become prosperous. If this is what you are thinking, you are missing the point. Maybe if you had five jobs, then you would have more money. You just would not sleep. No, this is not God's will. This is poverty thinking. I like to think of the example of a farmer with his crops growing while he sleeps at night. He works hard during the day, but his seed is growing in the nighttime while he is sleeping.

I love the scripture found in Ecclesiastes 2:26, "To the man who pleases him, God gives wisdom, knowledge and happiness, but to the sinner he gives the task of gathering and storing up wealth to hand it over to the one who pleases God. This too is meaningless, a chasing after the wind."

Peter Hartgerink is from Ottawa, Ontario, Canada. Here is his story:

> When I first heard this teaching on prosperity I was starting a new information technology consulting business. Over the next couple of years, I realized that God was speaking to me and telling me he wanted to prosper me both financially and spiritually. This was a new thought to me. Since then many things have changed in my life.
>
> When I began my business I thought of it only as a means of funding what I thought was my real ministry, which was church-planting. I have since

learned that I am better at business than I am at church-planting. That used to bother me but now I see that it's simply a matter of developing the areas in which God has given me grace instead of striving to be something I am not. I have learned to take a more entrepreneurial approach to life. I now see that managing finances with skill, wisdom, integrity and generosity is a godly calling. I want to be like Joseph, a man who can give out to others and sow funds into kingdom purposes because I have learned to steward finances faithfully and well.

The teaching in this book is one of the main influences that helped me to get to where I am today. I especially appreciate the emphasis on giving as a key to keeping our hearts free from materialism and greed.

Prosperity of soul will cause us to prosper in all areas. It is a revelation. It flows out from within us. It is not the result of our striving. What could Joseph have done to promote himself from slavery to the second highest government official in all of Egypt? It could not have happened by his own effort. The Holy Spirit is a patient teacher. There is a proverb that states the path of the righteous is like the dawning sun, shining brighter and brighter until the full day. Let faith for biblical prosperity grow inside of you and nothing will be able to contain it.

Teach me to prosper

Your finances are not the responsibility of the government, your family or the church. If you feel like a victim of fate, the lack of opportunities, the choices of others or circumstances beyond your control, I want to encourage you to take a fresh look at your situation. It might seem like you are in a hopeless, financial cycle and you cannot do anything to change it. It may feel like this is your lot in life. But you can do something to change your financial condition. Your finances are your responsibility. It is great if others help, but the responsibility is yours. You are the one who must believe in God as El Shaddai.

You are currently reaping what you have sown in your finances. Allow the Holy Spirit to show you what changes may be necessary. You will hear more of my story in the pages ahead. I am sure yours will be different, but just as exciting. Pause now and ask the Holy Spirit to teach you to prosper and let the adventure begin.

At this point you might say, "This is great theory, but how do I apply these truths to my life?" That's what we will look at in Part II of the book.

Small Group Study Questions

1. How can we change our thinking about our finances?

2. Give an example where the spirit of poverty might be influencing your life.

3. How can striving for riches keep us from having a prosperous soul?

4. If the Holy Spirit is a patient teacher, how will he teach us to prosper?

5. Pray this prayer: "Holy Spirit, teach me to prosper."

Part II

How Do I Get There From Here?

Chapter 7

Do You Have a Christian Worldview?

Do you have a Christian worldview? At first glance, some Christians might be slightly offended at this question. If you are offended, feel free to put this book down and continue on as you have been living. On the other hand, if you are willing to take the risk, perhaps we can help identify one of the handles that the spirit of poverty has used to ensnare you.

The spirit of poverty leaves us feeling like things will never change—that we can never get ahead and that we will always be at that same job, building widgets. "This is our place in life and that is the way it is," we tell ourselves. "Our finances will always be out of control. The money just keeps coming in and going out. Things will never change." This is called fatalism: There is no hope for change in the future. This is contrary to the Christian worldview.

If I were honest

To be honest, in the past I actually felt more spiritual or thought it was more spiritual to be in financial lack. I saw it as my cross to bear. In my mind, suffering for the sake of the gospel included not having sufficient or immediate resources. I was shocked to find that this mindset has more to do with a Hindu worldview than a Christian worldview. Listen to what Darrow L. Miller has to say in his book *Discipling Nations*:

> Hindu society actually values ignorance. Imagine you are a development worker who wants to teach poor people in India how to read and write. After all, you reason, illiterate people have little chance of improving their lives. Yet when you get there and begin to grasp the Hindu culture, it slowly dawns on you that in the Hindu system encouraging the poor to learn is asking them to sin. Hinduism, for its part, has no rationale for why people should be helped. This system asserts that the poor are the poor because of what they did in their past lives, and their quickest way out of poverty in the next life is to suffer in this one.[1]

By comparison, I realized the Christian worldview is one of advancing and growing. The Lord does not want me to languish in the same place in any area of my life. He desires to provide the necessary resources so there can be growth and increase in every area of our lives.

Picture with me the invalid man beside the pool of Bethesda who had been there for thirty-eight years. Healing was actually within his eyesight, but he was never able to get into the pool to receive it. It is very likely he saw others healed but never had a chance himself until Jesus came along one day. This is a prophetic picture of how the spirit of poverty paralyzes many Christians.

Having served as a youth pastor for a number of years, I found the study of world religions and a biblical worldview helped me to understand and answer the worldview questions of teenagers. If we look at world religions today, we find the idea of things never changing is more closely aligned to the Hindu worldview than the Christian worldview.

Miller states Hinduism has at its core the idea that a person is assigned a place in life. It sees perfection as a state of resignation and complacency. This causes people to withdraw from the world and not attack its evils. There is no hope or desire to change their present situation. There is no rationale for why people should be helped. The poor are poor because of what they did in their past lives, and the way out of poverty in the next life is to suffer in this one. The caste system in India is an example of a society in the grip of such Hindu fatalism. "Do not interfere with the workings of karma," we are told. "Leave the destitute in their state." It is not a coincidence that few advances in science, innovations and cures for diseases are coming out of Hindu India.

According to Miller this same fatalism—feeling like things will never change—is found in other non-Christian world religions. In Thailand for example, the peasant is labeled "jaak-con" meaning "destined to poverty." This attitude enslaves the poor in poverty. In some African languages there is not even a concept of "distant" future. This means there is not a category to define things getting better. In the heart of Buddhism is suffering and death. The goal of the Buddhist is not to combat suffering and death but to escape from them into a spiritual state.

In contrast the Christian worldview is one of advancement. Poverty is rooted in the rejection of Christianity. The gospel is good news. It brings self-respect and self-worth and causes people to desire to advance. Can we permanently settle in our minds that God wants us to advance? Although this thought is embedded in Western society, which has its origins in the Christian worldview, this is not an idea of Western society. It is a biblical, Christian idea.

In Alvin Schmidt's profound book *How Christianity Changed the World* [2] he documents the amazing advancement of society due to the influence of Christianity. Women were oppressed in cultures prior to the coming of Christianity. Slavery, which was quite common before Christianity, has been almost virtually eliminated from the civilized world. There was little interest in the poor, the sick and the dying until early Christians ministered to these needs. The first hospitals were started by Christians. Education came into maturity under the influence of Christianity. The commandment against stealing redefined the concept of private property and property rights. The rise of modern science has been directly linked with the biblical understanding of the world. Schmidt documents and gives hundreds of examples of how Christianity has caused society to advance.

A few years ago we moved into a house that had more room for our growing family. It was not a new house so most of the appliances had been there for a number of years. One day after church, my wife told me the oven stopped working. We were having people over for lunch so we went to plan B, and I cooked the meat on the grill. From that time on my wife and I resigned ourselves not to use the oven again. I guess it's not God's will for us to have an oven. Is that how we responded? No! What is our intuitive response when something like this happens? Get it fixed or get a new one. We got a new one, better than the old one and added a microwave too. In addition, we did a lot more improvements to the house to make it better. This is an example of an advancing mindset.

Understand that God wants you to advance

We only have to look at the beginning of the Bible to find out God's heart on this. We discover that soon after Adam and Eve were put on the earth, they were commissioned to advance and bear fruit.

> God blessed them and said to them, "Be fruitful and increase in number; fill the earth and subdue it. Rule over the fish of the sea and the birds of the air and over every living creature that moves on the ground" (Genesis 1:28).

Be fruitful! In contrast, the spirit of poverty makes us feel trapped where we are. God does want us to advance. Take the promotion at your job. Start taking classes to get a better job. If we have an advancing mindset, our current financial situation does not matter. Think of Joseph's prosperous soul regardless of his circumstances. We cannot just wish we had a better job; we need to take steps to get one. We observe that Adam and Eve were quickly assigned the task of naming the animals. They were not to let things the way they were but to bring advancement.

Consider this: God is a loving Father who creates unfinished things so those he loves may have a meaningful existence, purpose and a sense of accomplishment in life. For example God created corn but he leaves it up to us to put it in rows and feed the world with it as stated in Psalm 104:14.

> He makes grass grow for the cattle, and plants for
> man to cultivate—bringing forth food from the earth.

He created everything to grow and reproduce. Again in Genesis we find that God created plants that produced after their own kind—plants with seeds in them and fruit with seeds. This is a part of his divine nature that he wants us to take part in. It is his will for us to advance. People without an advancing mindset will not innovate and improve their life. In certain parts of the world that lack a Christian worldview, villagers will carry buckets of water for miles each day. They will do this for many years without ever attempting to dig a well in the place where they live.

What was it that caused Wilbur and Orville Wright to want to fly and discover the laws of flight and the airplane? Were they just bored with the train, or was there something in the hearts of these two Christian men that caused them to want to advance? And look at what has happened since then. The entire first flight of the Kitty Hawk was a shorter distance than the wingspan of a modern 747 jet. Amazing.

Oil is an energy form that is limited, but we find we can develop new sources like the wind and the sun that are not limited. Somehow we are no longer limited to the use of telephone wires for communication. No, we found something better, like fiber optics, which is an improvement and then wireless technology which is a greater improvement. Dennis Peacocke has made these profound observations.

> Poverty is rooted in the rejection of Christianity, its
> view of reality, and its discipline. Without the founda-
> tions of the biblical worldview, society's attempts to

alleviate poverty are doomed.... Poverty is a spiritual problem more than an economic one. Paganism produces poverty; obedience to God's covenant produces wealth.

People who do not live in a covenant with their Creator will not invest in the future, because it is too unpredictable. Instead, they will live in constant fear of the future. That is why free enterprise systems flourish only where the biblical worldview flourishes. Prosperity comes to societies where people invest current resources in the future; and this best happens when people trust the faithfulness (predictability) of a covenant-keeping God who promises to reward your investment if you invest, work hard and obey Him.[3]

It is a waste to think small, sit still, do nothing, not invest, go nowhere and refuse to enjoy life. A prosperous soul acts, gives, blesses, goes, enjoys life and receives it all from God! To live life just to pay your bills is to live a life of selfish underachieving.

Is it okay to change jobs?

A lot of times a spirit of poverty in our lives will make us feel like we are locked into the same job. It is important for us to notice that some jobs pay more than others. This may seem obvious to some, but others cannot see it because of the blinding effects of the spirit of poverty. Let's take a blunt look at reality—people are not paid for how hard they work; it's what type of work they do. For example, ditch diggers work physically harder than lawyers, but lawyers make significantly more money. Though this is a very simple concept, I only received a revelation of this a few years ago. It changed my thinking and gave me some fresh insight that has helped many others.

I realized right away this was a principle I wanted to teach my children. My teenage son had a job cleaning up an upholstery shop on the weekends. He also had another part-time job where he operated a television camera. He was paid five dollars more per hour to operate the television camera, although it was a much less strenuous job. This was an easy lesson for him to see.

Sometimes Christians tell me they are considering a new job and ask for my advice about taking the new job. Unless I am directed otherwise by the Lord, my first question is always to inquire if the new job pays more than the one they now have. If so, I often point out that it is likely God's will for them to advance into this new position. This is usually a relief to them because a lot of times they feel guilty about getting paid more or are concerned about their co-workers to whom they have been witnessing. I generally assure them that God can still reach their co-workers even without them there.

In today's society, it is quite common for people to change careers four or five times in their lifetime and it is okay to do this. Consider going back to school for some more training. Improve yourself and you will be a better employee or qualify for a promotion. You are not locked into your current position.

It is essential that you believe in yourself. It's the poverty mindset that says you cannot change. It is the poverty mindset that tells you that you are too old to go back to school and change jobs. If you believe you are worth more per hour, then others will start to believe it, and usually over a period of time you will get paid more per hour. Does this mean that everyone should change jobs? No, if you are in a low-paying employment situation, decide if that is where God wants you to be. Are you content there? If not, you will not prosper there. If the people you are working beside are not accumulating money, neither will you. Be prepared though—changing careers does take time.

One of the boards on which I serve is involved with microfinance in developing countries of the world. Without going into a lot of detail, one of the reasons I love this concept is because it is helping people break out of a poverty mindset where there are no jobs available. It is helping them to create their own jobs. It is helping them to advance.

Is living paycheck-to-paycheck God's will? We will take more time on that later, but for now, be convinced that God wants you to advance. Sometimes when I teach on advancing, people will misunderstand and say, "Oh, I'll have to get a second job to become more prosperous." This is not it. God might have a better job for you, but it does not mean working twice or three times as hard.

I live in the middle of rich Pennsylvania farmland. A farmer in our area constantly worked his equipment with the throttle wide open. He drove from the barn to the field as fast as he could. Another wise, prosperous farmer predicted this farmer would never be able to make any money because his equipment was not designed to run full throttle and would not last. A few years later, the first farmer had to sell his farm and take another job. He could never get ahead because his equipment kept wearing out.

Our bodies were not made to be running at full throttle eighteen hours a day, seven days a week. God has a path of blessing for you to walk in. Let Him do it. Let the Word of God cause faith to rise in your heart to embrace El Shaddai and your expectation of God's financial provision of more than enough. Expect him to teach you to prosper. Allow him to change your beliefs. If your patterns of thinking change, the words that you speak will begin to change. If your words change, your actions will change. And, if your actions change, the outcome will change.

God wants to change our thinking about what to expect. Remember the apostle John's words to Gauis, "as your soul prospers, you will prosper." If we perceive and embrace this truth in our hearts, nothing can stop it from flowing out.

NOTES

1   Darrow L. Miller, *Discipling Nations* (Washington: YWAM Publishing, 1998), 68.
2   Alvin J. Schmidt, *How Christianity Changed the World (Michigan*: Zondervan, 2004).
3   Dennis Peacocke, (California: Strategic Christian Services, 1995). Used by permission.

Small Group Study Questions

1. What is the difference between the Hindu and Christian worldview?

2. Define fatalism.

3. How has Christianity changed the world?

4. What was it that caused Joseph to advance?

5. Explain this statement: People are not paid for how hard they work, it's what type of work they do.

Chapter 8

How God Advances Us

Recently, I was privileged to hear a wealthy man speaking with some servicemen and women who were wounded in combat. He was talking about possessing courage to take risks. Interestingly, he spoke about financial courage as being different than other kinds of courage. When stating that he had the confidence to take financial risks, he qualified that statement by saying it would be difficult for him to risk his life on a battlefield. He said he did not possess that kind of courage. I learned something that day. There are different types of courage.

It is interesting to me that you could have so much courage in one area but not in another. But this is really true. A construction worker can have the courage to balance himself on a six-inch I-beam, hundreds of feet above the ground, but at the same time not have the courage to stand up in front of a group of forty people and give a speech or walk into the bank to meet with the bank manager to talk about financing a project. Likewise, a salesman who has the courage to knock on a dozen doors a day making sales calls might not have the financial courage to buy a single share of stock.

There are different kinds of courage. We need courage in the financial area. With God's help we can obtain the financial courage and strategy that we need to walk in the prosperity that he has for us. There are specific things we can do to help us become more comfortable in the financial world. We must learn to overcome the misconceptions we have about the financial world and how it functions.

Do not expect to get rich quick

Do not look for the big break, the miraculous provision, the chance deal, an inheritance or the lottery to get rich quick. In a few words, the desire to get rich quick is really an ungodly lust for financial success without learning how to manage money. If we can get this concept into our minds, we will be far closer to learning how God wants to advance us.

Advancement comes to those who diligently apply God's principles on a consistent, long-term basis. Look for steady progress through diligent, consistent work. God generally advances us gradually so we can concurrently grow the maturity to hold on to what he gives us. It is like a plane taking off—there is a correct trajectory of climbing that will not stall the plane's motor and yet gets you in the air before the end of the runway. Eyes set on the "chance that may come" will keep you from taking today's step forward. Proverbs speaks to the trap of sitting around and waiting for your ship to come in.

He who works his land will have abundant food, but the one who chases fantasies will have his fill of poverty. A faithful man will be richly blessed, but one eager to get rich will not go unpunished (Proverbs 28:19–20).

A minister friend of mine calls this get rich quick mentality "lottery thinking." I have to agree with him, lottery thinking is poverty thinking. The people who spend the most money on lottery tickets are at the bottom of the income scale. When politicians start a lottery to fund a government project, they generally consider it a tax on the poor. The help you need is not a big sum of money dumped in your lap, but rather a kick in the pants to start moving so God can bless your steps of faith.

What if you win the lottery, so what? You still will not have wisdom to manage money. If you gain something without growing into it, you will find it slipping through your fingers.

Of what use is money in the hand of a fool, since he has no desire to get wisdom? (Proverbs 17:16).

To see this, consider what happens to people who actually have won a lottery and received the amount in one large lump sum. Studies which follow their lives reveal that within ten years, they typically are financially broke, have had extramarital affairs, gotten divorced, and many have become addicted to drugs and have destroyed most of their relationships with family and friends. Sadly, a significant number of them commit suicide.

I know a businessman who once said, "We will not win the lottery. If you see money falling out of the sky, it is counterfeit;

do not pick it up!" Pastors and church leaders can fall into lottery thinking with their churches. They will set their eye on the "big fish" to build their churches. They become event oriented, thinking that if they can just have the right speaker or music group it will cause the church to grow. Events do not grow churches. Consistent, diligent work and prayer does. An event will draw a crowd for a weekend, but without day-to-day nurture and outreach the crowds will quickly disappear. If you build systematically, God will bring the growth. The answer is not out there somewhere; it is right in front of you with the step forward God wants you to take today.

Other pastors may think if someone in a wheelchair is healed, it will cause their church to grow. This fixation on a spectacular event can immobilize them from doing the things that will make the church grow and maybe eventually see a person in the wheelchair healed. God's normal way is the way of gradual, sure, systematic growth and maturity. God's nature is seed time and harvest. According to Hebrews 6, it is through faith and patience that we receive from God.

> We do not want you to become lazy, but to imitate
> those who through faith and patience inherit what has
> been promised (Hebrews 6:12).

Job's patience was what helped him overcome the hardships he faced when he was attacked by the enemy. Patience is much more than just the ability not to become angry in a difficult situation. Patience is the power that will carry you through the obstacles of life into the seasons of blessing. It is notable that sometimes a wealthy person will lose all of their money, but somehow they seem to earn it all back, and more. Amazingly enough, this was Job's experience. Let's examine some more scriptures:

> Dishonest money dwindles away, but he who gathers money little by little makes it grow.... All hard work brings a profit, but mere talk leads only to poverty...The path of the righteous is like the first gleam of dawn, shining ever brighter till the full light of day...An inheritance quickly gained at the beginning will not be blessed at the end (Proverbs 13:11; 14:23, 4:18, 20:21).

Can you pick up the pattern here? Gather money little by little … hard work brings profit … shining ever brighter until the full light of day … inheritance gained quickly will not be blessed. Listen to Russell Conwell's analysis of getting a large inheritance. He considered it to be a curse.

> The moment a young man or woman gets more money than he or she has grown by practical experience is the moment he has gotten a curse. It is no help to a young man or woman to inherit money. It is no help to your children to leave them money, but if you leave them education, if you leave them Christian and noble character, if you leave them a wide circle of friends, if you leave them an honorable name, it is far better than that they should have money. It would be worse for them, worse for the nation, that they should have any money at all. Oh, young man, if you have inherited money, do not regard it as a help. It will

curse you through your years, and deprive you of the very best things of human life. There is no class of people to be pitied so much as the inexperienced sons and daughters of the rich of our generation. I pity the rich man's son. He can never know the best things in life.

If we are sitting around waiting for an inheritance or hoping for an insurance settlement, we will not prosper. If our eyes are set on the chance that may come, it will keep us from taking today's step forward. Listen to how the *Living Bible* translates Habakkuk 2:3:

Slowly, steadily surely the time approaches when the vision will be fulfilled, do not despair for these things will surely come to pass. Just be patient, they will not be overdue a single day.

A prosperous soul will begin wherever it is and work toward advancement. Progress, God's blessing, raises, promotions and favor are expected, but faithfulness and steady progress are the path to get there.

It is okay to talk about money

In order for us to develop some financial courage we will have to get over the idea that it is not spiritual to talk about money. People afflicted by the spirit of poverty find it difficult to talk about money. A lot of churches struggle to communicate financial needs or even to take a biblical offering for a need or vision the church is undertaking. Jesus spoke about money a lot. There are more than three-thousand references to money in the Bible. People with a poverty spirit did not like to talk about money. On the other hand, prosperous people enjoy talking about money.

> But remember the Lord your God, for it is he who
> gives you the ability to produce wealth, and so con-
> firms his covenant, which he swore to your forefathers,
> as it is today (Deuteronomy 8:18).

So let's take a closer look at this. You mean God gives us the power and creativity to get wealth, but we are not supposed to talk about it? No, it is OK to talk about money. Certainly we need to keep money in its proper perspective. To prosperous people money is important and interesting. They enjoy talking about and learning about money. They are unashamed to have a good conversation with their children and friends about the ins and outs of money. How are we going to learn about managing money without talking about it?

Do not shrink back from talking to your children about money. Teach them to earn, tithe, give and save. As insecure parents we mistakenly tell our children we cannot afford something instead of having the courage to say "no" to things they are requesting. The truth is you could afford what they are asking for, but you have decided to spend that money on something else. Just tell them no, they cannot have the item. It will be a good life lesson for them.

The wealthy

The final example stems from a book that I believe God directed me to read. The title of the book is *The Millionaire Next*

Door. This book basically studied the wealthy in America and examined their lifestyles. The main point of the book is that most wealthy people look like (and probably are) the people who are your neighbors. Its research showed that most of the wealthy were married with kids and did not inherit vast sums of money. They still work fifty hours per week, live below their means and wear inexpensive suits. Their wealth came by working and saving and investing 20 percent of their income. In most cases they worked most of their lives to become wealthy and did not drive exotic foreign cars. In fact, the book revealed that most of the people who drive exotic foreign cars are not wealthy at all. In essence, most of the wealthy look and act like our neighbor next door.[2]

The statistics from the book helped me because in my mind, I had this fixation that to be wealthy meant you had to be showy and vain like many movie stars and professional athletes. I changed my wrong perception of what it "looked like" to be wealthy. God has a better way. The Bible teaches something different about God's blessing.

This is the truth. It helps us know how to have a healthy attitude toward money. Let's be free to talk openly and honestly about money. On the other hand, some Christians have accumulated wealth and yet act as if they have nothing. I do not believe this is a biblical and healthy approach to money either. Proverbs 13:7 says: One man pretends to be rich, yet has nothing; another pretends to be poor, yet has great wealth.

Let's just be honest. Money helps us do what we are called to do to expand the kingdom of God. Money is not evil unless we fall in love with it. It is a tool. We can and should learn from others who have financial courage so we can develop it in our lives.

Learn from prosperous people

Let me encourage you to try an experiment. At your next extended family dinner ask a relative who is prosperous what was the best financial decision they have ever made. This will do two things. It will help you break out of the fear of talking about money, and likely you will hear some financial information that will help you. If we ask and observe who is around us, it is likely that the Lord will provide some financial mentors for us. It will feel uncomfortable at first, but you will develop confidence and find who is willing to help you. Most financially prosperous people will take it as a compliment that you want to learn from the wisdom they have. Proverbs connects "not learning" with poverty. We must be willing to learn:

> He who ignores discipline comes to poverty and shame, but whoever heeds correction is honored ... let the wise listen and add to their learning, and let the discerning get guidance (Proverbs 13:18, 1:5).

Wealth is not evil, so lose your attitude toward wealthy people. This attitude is rooted in envy and jealousy. Envy and jealousy are sin. In his book *Breaking the Power of Evil*, Rick Joyner says,

> One of the biggest open doors that the spirit of poverty has into our lives is through our own unrighteous judgments.... I once visited a state that was under one of the most powerful spirits of poverty that I have witnessed in this country. It was remarkable because it is a state of great beauty and natural resources. It had talented and resourceful people, but a spirit of poverty

was on almost everyone. Another characteristic that stood out was that almost everyone I met there seemed to uncontrollably scorn and criticize anyone who was prosperous or powerful.

With every pastor of a small church whom I met (and almost all of the churches in this state were very small), the conversation would inevitably turn to criticizing "mega-churches" and "mega-ministries," which these people obviously thought were the reason for many of their own problems. What made the situation even sadder was that many of these small-church pastors were called to walk in much more authority than the leaders of the large churches or ministries that they criticized.

Many pastors yoke themselves and their congregations to financial poverty by criticizing how other churches or ministries take up offerings or solicit donations. Because of their judgment of others, they then cannot even take up a biblical offering without feeling guilty. They have yoked themselves by their unrighteous judgment[3].

Most wealthy people have some financial wisdom we could use. Our judgments against them erect a wall that will keep us from becoming like them. Remember in the U.S., most millionaires still work fifty hours a week and did not inherit their money. They have financial wisdom. Ask prosperous people for advice. Find someone who has victory in a financial area that you are lacking and ask them for help. Jesus said you would be like your teachers, so ask someone to help you with a budget or to go to see the bank manager. It is wise to ask for help.

At first, the financial world will seem too complex, too hard to learn, too many new words to learn and too overwhelming. This is a barrier erected by the spirit of poverty. Do not quit. Persevere. You can do it. Buy a financial magazine or the "Wall Street Journal." Start to learn.

Author Harold Eberle from Yakama, Washington says it this way, "You learned to drive a car, you can learn about money. In fact, learning about money is more important to success in life than learning how to drive a car. If you learn about money, you can hire someone else to drive a car for you."

God wants to advance us. Let's get some financial courage, learn from others and take some steps ahead. He will help us.

NOTES

1   Russell Cronwell, *Acres of Diamonds* (Pennsylvania: Temple University).
2   Thomas J. Stanley, *The Millionaire Next Door* (New York: Pocket, 1996).
3   Rick Joyner, *Breaking the Power of Evil: Winning the Battle for the Soul of Man* (Pennsylvania: Destiny Image Publishers, 2002).

Small Group Study Questions

1. Explain financial courage.

2. What is lottery thinking?

3. How can we learn from prosperous people?

4. Why should we talk to children about money?

5. How is lack of learning related to poverty?

CHAPTER 9

Does God Help Those Who Help Themselves?

In the movie *Facing the Giants* there is a conversation about two farmers who were praying for rain for their crops. Both farmers were asking God for rain, but one farmer was digging irrigation ditches while the other was sitting in his house waiting for the rain to come. The question was asked, "Which farmer has more faith?" Without getting into a huge theological discussion, I have come to realize that God does expect us to put some action to our faith. This is a change from the way I once thought, and I would now say it is a more prosperous way of thinking.

Many years ago when I first heard the statement, "God helps those who help themselves," I reacted to it negatively. In my passionate spirituality I said categorically that this was just an excuse to rely on human effort instead of God. I told the individual that nowhere in the Bible does it say that God helps those that help themselves. I have changed my mind and had to eat these words that I thought were so spiritual. I humbly intend to show you in this chapter how God does help those who help themselves.

Christians are fond of quoting and praying the scriptures that state the wealth of the wicked is stored up for the righteous as stated in Proverbs 13:22. I believe these scriptures are absolutely true; however, I am not sure that God will automatically transfer wealth to his children in the last days. This expectation appears to be based on faith, but it sounds a lot like lottery thinking. As we will see in a moment from looking at Elisha's interaction with a widow, faith without works is dead. The Lord expects us to be active participants in receiving the wealth of the wicked. It is a joint venture.

Prepare and take action

Let me ask a question. Would you allow someone to manage your financial accounts and personal savings who is personally in debt, has never themselves saved money, accumulated wealth or managed property? I'm guessing you would not. Why then do we expect the Lord to just dump money in our laps without us ever learning the principles of finance and money management? He expects us to prepare and take action.

When Elisha encountered the widow woman who was in serious financial need, he did not, to use today's terminology, just write her a check. She was a godly woman who was in desperate need, but he still asked her to participate with him in the financial blessings he was about to release. This is a picture of how God the Father asks us to participate in receiving from him today. It is interesting to note that Elisha required the widow woman to collect vessels to contain the oil that was to be poured out, and she was rewarded according to her level of participation. If she had gathered more containers, she would have gotten more financial reward. Interesting. Can we be motivated to work and prepare for God's blessing?

The Bible states the most amazing thing about Hezekiah. The simple truth of this Bible passage has revolutionized my life especially in the area of finances.

> This is what Hezekiah did throughout Judah, doing what was good and right and faithful before the Lord his God. In everything that he undertook in the service of God's temple and in obedience to the law and the commands, he sought his God and worked wholeheartedly. And so he prospered (2 Chronicles 31:20–21).

Hezekiah sought his God. He worked wholeheartedly and so he prospered. After stating what Hezekiah did was good and right and faithful, we are given his methodology that was so pleasing to God. Can we do the same? First, seek the Lord earnestly in prayer, then apply all of our spirit, soul and body to the task at hand, be it financial or otherwise, and then expect God's prosperity will follow. It is a simple, practical three-step process, and I have found that it works.

We find the same thing when we look at churches. Some churches spend their time praying and some churches spend their time doing. Which is correct? Actually both are needed and correct but not at the expense of the other. Should a church pray for the lost to come to faith in Christ? Absolutely. However, at a certain time the church leadership should focus on training the church members in evangelism and provide opportunities for them to evangelize.

On the other side of the coin, should a church that wants to do successful evangelism just expect that God will bless their evangelistic efforts without prayer? Of course not; they should pray fervently before, during and after the evangelism outreach. They are correct in doing and they are correct in praying, and just like Hezekiah, they can expect the Lord to bless their efforts. Proverbs states that it is both the fruit of our lips (our prayers and declarations) and the work of our hands that reward us.

> From the fruit of his lips a man is filled with good
> things as surely as the work of his hands rewards him
> (Proverbs 12:14).

This scripture alone could revolutionize your life. Pray and do. We will look at this again from another angle when we discuss the importance of our words.

Dig ditches

In 2 Kings 3, we have the historical account of the kings of Israel and Judah marching out into the desert on the way to fight the King of Moab. They ran out of water and inquired of Elisha the prophet about what they should do. He told them they should dig ditches and God would fill them with water. Let's look at the story.

> While the harpist was playing, the hand of the
> Lord came upon Elisha and he said, "This is what the
> Lord says: Make this valley full of ditches. For this
> is what the Lord says: You will see neither wind nor
> rain, yet this valley will be filled with water, and you,

your cattle and your other animals will drink. This
is an easy thing in the eyes of the Lord; he will also
hand Moab over to you...." The next morning, about
the time for offering the sacrifice, there it was—water
flowing from the direction of Edom! And the land was
filled with water (2 Kings 3:15–19, 20).

We see again that the Lord expected some action from the
kings of Israel and Judah to match his efforts. We should do things
to put ourselves in a place for God to prosper us. Dr. Thomas
Anderson describes how it worked for the children of Israel as
they entered the Promised Land:

But with abundance comes a need to learn how to
produce wealth. God blessed their work, but they had
to work, and not just hard but also smart. They had to
know some things. The Promised Land flowed with
milk and honey, but to get milk from a cow, they had
to know how to milk a cow and they had to have the
self discipline to actually go out and milk it everyday.
To get honey they had to learn something about bees.
God's people too often think that all they have to do
is confess prosperity and wait for it to come. God
said he would teach us how to produce wealth, and
that he would bless our efforts, but we still have to
do something to produce it (Deuteronomy 29:9; 30:9;
James 2:17)[1].

As we have previously examined, the children of Israel had
manna come from heaven while they were wandering in the wil-

derness, but later they were expected to work, sow and reap in the Promised Land. Is God going to drop money out of heaven like he did manna in the wilderness? Not usually, this would only cultivate a lazy spirit. God helps and rewards those who take initiative. There are times God tells us to wait, but most of the time he expects us to act. Dr. Anderson gives the example of Solomon and how God gave him wisdom.

> Solomon asked God for wisdom but to achieve it, he still had to read and study and learn. Solomon did not just sit down one day and start writing Proverbs. Many of the things in that book can be traced to older books of wisdom in other cultures, especially Egypt. Solomon studied them and compiled them adding his own insights as he went. Such study is an integral part of becoming wise. When you attain wisdom, the world will seek you out to ask advice[2].

Our tendency is to just read Proverbs and think that it was a download from God. This is probably not the way it happened. It was from God, but it also involved study, practice and the life experiences of Solomon. Do you think Solomon tried things that did not work? Of course he did, he made many mistakes. So, as we read the following proverbs related to this topic we know this was not just theory but the product of study and life experiences.

> He who works his land will have abundant food, but he who chases fantasies lacks judgment. The slug-gard craves and gets nothing, but the desires of the diligent are fully satisfied. Lazy hands make a man poor, but diligent hands bring wealth. He who gath-

ers crops in summer is a wise son, but he who sleeps during harvest is a disgraceful son (Proverbs 12:11; 13:4; 10:4-5).

It is as simple as this. We will not have a business unless we start one. We will not own stock unless we buy some. We will not own real estate unless we go through the process to purchase some. We will never know if our wild idea for a service or a product is a good one until we try it, first on ourselves and then on others. We can have the best product in the world, but if no one knows about it via our marketing, no one can purchase it. We will never write a book unless we get a computer and start typing. Listen to this quote from author Dennis Peacock:

Laziness is married to poverty. Wealth is produced by work. If people did not work, they did not create wealth. Those who did not create wealth become dependent on others for survival[3].

Close to the end of Paul's first letter to the Christians at Thessalonica is this statement, "Warn those who are idle." Apparently, some of the believers were so sure of the imminent return of Jesus that they gave up their jobs in order to prepare for his return. Paul was not impressed with this approach. He felt they should work. To Paul, work was spiritual.

Financial dominion

We will have to learn to take dominion over our finances and make financial decisions from a place of confidence. A king has dominion over his kingdom, so for us to have dominion over our finances means we have authority and rule over them. At the same time we cannot ignore the natural wisdom and talents that God has given us to use in accumulating data to make a good decision. As I have spent time with prosperous people, I have found they act according to a "gut" feeling they have developed because of life experiences.

We cannot rush financial decisions. Let emotional excitement pass (like after talking to a salesman) and wait until you have a sense of dominion (confidence) within. Wait until the next day. When someone presents me with an opportunity that I have to decide on immediately, the answer is a simple, "no." I would rather miss an opportunity than be pushed into making a decision I am not comfortable with, especially if there is not time to consult with my discerning wife. God is big enough to provide other opportunities.

Financial dominion means you are not over-extending yourself. Do not get in over your head. Start small. Jesus came to the earth as a baby and it took thirty-three years to accomplish his purpose. Do not be anxious. Ask for advice. Do not make a decision in a vacuum. To do anything beyond what you have confidence to do is risky. Do what feels right and gives you peace, not in your emotions but in your gut. You might have peace in your heart to take financial risks that others do not. Others might have peace to take financial risks that you do not. Go with what is in your heart.

We work so that God can bless the work of our hand. Doing our part is like putting a lightning rod in the ground. When God sends lightning we are going to receive it. However if we never put a lightning rod in the ground, we will never receive the lightning we are looking for. Remember our study of Joseph, he did his part, but the hand of God was on him to promote him. How about Queen Esther interceding for the children of Israel? Was it only God's favor that put her in that position? No, her natural beauty and a time of preparation put her in the position to one day intercede and save her people. It was the natural and the supernatural.

If you want to be fisherman, you cannot live in Iowa. For those of you reading outside of the United States, Iowa is landlocked in the middle of the country. If we want to catch fish, we have to at least position ourselves on or around water. To be fair, Iowa does have some lakes and rivers where you can fish; however you get the point—God expects us to do our part. My wife and I own one business and are part owners of another business. God is blessing us financially through these businesses, but we had to take the steps to get into them. Believe me they were steps of faith and practical tasks as well. It is faith and works. Here is Dr. Anderson's view of our responsibility in this divine partnership.

> There are no shortcuts to great wealth. When you try to find easy money, you actually rob yourself of many of the lessons that you need for success. You must learn discipline, passion, generosity and creativity. The world determines wealth and success by what you have. God determines wealth and success by what you give. Success is about what you become. You must develop the character to own your possessions or they will own you[4].

God generally does not drop money out of heaven (as he did manna in the wilderness). He is not going to counterfeit it. No

... to enter abundance you have to make change! We will discuss the practical aspects of this later, but first we have to understand God's economy.

NOTES

1   Dr. C. Thomas Anderson, *Becoming a Millionaire God's Way* (New York: Faith Words, Hachette Book Group, 2006).
2   Ibid., 60
3   Dennis Peacocke, (California: Strategic Christian Services, Newsletter, 1995). Used by permission.

4   Dr. C. Thomas Anderson, *Becoming a Millionaire God's Way* (New York: Faith Words, Hachette Book Group, 2006), p.xvi

Small Group Study Questions

1.   How does God help those who help themselves?

2.   Describe how Elisha interacted with the widow.

3.   Describe the simple process Hezekiah followed.

4.   How are work and wealth related?

5.   What is financial dominion?

Chapter 10

God's Economy

A few years ago, on very short notice, the church we attend lost the lease on the property it was using. With only a few thousand dollars in the building fund, the church was looking at close to one-hundred-thousand dollars needed to renovate the only property that was available on such short notice. I was an elder in the church at the time and remember distinctly the elders discussing what should be done. One elder, my wife, suggested we treat the few thousand we had as seed and sow most of it into a mission agency's building project.

After getting over the initial shock of this suggestion, everyone in the room swallowed hard and knew it was the right thing to do, and that was the decision that was made. The little bit of money in the building fund was given away. God honored that seed and a few months later, we moved into the newly renovated building with almost all the costs paid for in cash. Giving is central to God's economy.

Financial funnel

One time I was praying in my home, and God showed me a brief picture of myself as a funnel for finances. There were resources coming to me from a wide spectrum of sources and then as they came under the influence of my "kingdom of God" mentality, I would redirect them to the place where they were needed to expand the kingdom. This was a very vivid picture that has stayed with me to this day. Picture yourself as a funnel with money coming in from many sources. As the money passes through your hands and comes under your authority, you have the opportunity to channel or direct it to extend the kingdom of God.

Our money literally represents our time and our talents. When we work and receive a paycheck, or invest our time and energy to increase the value of something to sell, it is the product of our efforts. It represents us. So when we give money away it is like giving something of ourselves away. Jesus literally sat by the money box in the synagogue watching what people gave. I believe he is still watching today to see what people give.

Do you remember the one hundred dollar bill story? I realized that God would take me seriously in expecting to receive one hundred dollar bills from him if I would take him seriously in expecting me to give away one hundred dollar bills. God is not afraid to talk about money in his word and his desire to bless us; however, he expects us to uphold our part of the bargain, which is central to his economy. He entrusts to us the opportunity to learn and understand his economy of giving.

Inflow

Right now, let's picture money flowing to you from many sources similar to how tributaries feed a river. A lot of Christians look only to paychecks as their source of income. Your salary is different from your income. Someone else, like your employer, might set your salary; however, you did not have to be satisfied or limited to that level of income. Your limited thinking can limit God's ability to open new sources. He might open up many other sources if we let him. Raise your faith and break through that ceiling of your salary level. Begin to pray and expect more income. We must understand that all the money that comes to us comes from God. The following is what I pray on a regular basis for finances to flow to me from multiple sources.

> "I am a money magnet. I receive salaries, raises, inheritances, dividends, discounts, bonuses, capital gains, royalties, book sales, honorariums, gifts, tax breaks, interests, rents, refunds, prizes, real estate appreciation, residuals, rebates, scholarships, firstfruits and offerings in Jesus' name. Money comes to me like water flows downhill."

A prayer like this might seem a bit audacious; however, I would point out that to date, I have received money from all but one of these sources and I expect that one will eventually open up. There might be some that I am missing that you might want to pray for yourself.

Outflow

This is the fun part. As the money passes through your hands, you have the opportunity to re-direct it to extend the kingdom of God. First, you must intentionally possess and own it. It is now under your authority. Remember, money will come to you from many sources, so you really do not know the history of it and what it was used for before it came to you. It might have been used for ungodly purposes. The scriptures do say that the wealth of the wicked is stored up for the righteous, so we can expect it might need some cleansing when it comes to us. It really does not matter where it came from, because now it will be used for the kingdom. This is why it is important that you take authority over it and earmark it for the kingdom of God. Doing this, is like cleansing it or sanctifying it for kingdom use.

When I say this, I am not talking about some kind of ceremony where we actually put all the money we receive in a physical pile and pray some kind of blessing or sprinkle holy water over it. No, I am talking about how you posture your heart and take dominion over the money you receive. It is a matter of faith and authority, this money has come under your authority. It will now be used for kingdom purposes. The following is my outflow prayer that I pray on a regular basis.

> "I tithe to my church and give to missionaries, building funds, training schools, church planters, educating the poor, feeding the poor, translation projects, revolving loan funds for the jobless, orphanages, micro-finance funds and well drilling for the thirsty in Jesus' name."

Your outflow will be different than mine depending on what the Lord has placed upon your heart. Let's get to the practical aspects of God's economy.

Give to God

The pain in my friend's face was obvious as he explained the dilemma he was facing. He and his wife were discipling another couple in their small group who had major issues in their finances. They felt like God had told them to financially help this struggling family and yet many of their financial decisions were ill-advised decisions with which my friend could not agree. They were now struggling with God asking them to give money to this couple who would spend it differently than they would.

My response was indicative of how we must see God's economy. I told my friend that even though their check was physically going from them to this other family, their giving was to God. This gave them the freedom to obey God and give the money as an offering to the Lord. Those who received the finances were accountable to God for how it was used.

Picture this with me: the check, cash, direct deposit or whatever we are giving actually travels horizontally (into the offering plate or charity), but all our giving is vertical (to God). For example, my wife and I might be sending a check to a ministry that is providing food and education for a needy child in Central America (horizontal); however, we consider the giving of this gift as to the Lord (vertical). We see all giving as giving to God.

Likewise, the money we receive from many sources in practicality is received horizontally into our hands: paycheck, dividends, gifts and so forth, but we keep the perspective that it comes vertically from the Lord above. This picture of God's economy has helped us keep our finances in a joy-filled perspective.

Give, Give, Give

As stated previously, the core of God's economy is giving. Give every opportunity you get. Give! Give! Give to everything you can. I encourage people to go through their possessions on a regular basis and give things away that they are not using. Never let an offering go by that you did not put something in. If you did not have cash or your checkbook, put your pen or pencil in the offering or tear a button off your shirt and put it in. Abraham was blessed to be a blessing and you are too. Be generous with your family, bless your kids, bless your waitress and bless your enemies.

> One man gives freely, yet gains even more; another withholds unduly, but comes to poverty. A generous man will prosper; he who refreshes others will himself be refreshed (Proverbs 11: 24–25).

Give your best

I glanced into the freezer in the garage as we were loading the car with our family to go to our church's small group meeting. My wife had just suggested that we take some ice cream along to serve after the meeting. Before me were two boxes of ice cream, one generic brand and one that was more expensive and richer tasting. In a split second I needed to decide which one to take. I realized that to give our best, we should take the more expensive ice cream. It was less than a dollar difference, but it is a principle we want to live by. I grabbed the more expensive box.

Why should we give our best? God gave his best when he gave his Son. If you think about it, when he was deciding how to save the world, God could have sent an angel instead of his son. It meant more to us because he gave his best. We should do likewise when we give. Remember the terminology of John 3:16, "For God so love the world that he gave...." When we give our best, we are acting like him. This is how someone made in his image and filled with his Spirit should live. This is the very nature of God, and it will make us more prosperous when we give our best.

Give more than you have given before

Since I teach on biblical prosperity people ask me all kinds of random questions about money. Someone asked me if I thought it was okay to spend a certain amount of money on a recreational item. My challenge to them was to hear from God about the purchase, but also to consider, have they ever given that much money away in a one-time gift? In other words, have they ever given away the same amount of money they were planning to spend on the recreational item in a one-time gift to fund the kingdom of God?

This might be a good standard of measure, but I believe the Lord would be grieved if my suggestion became some kind of a legalistic rule people are required to follow. For some, it may be a practical benchmark to consider.

I sometimes encourage people to use the "one time gift" after their local church tithe as a method to challenge themselves. If you have never given twenty-five dollars away, then stretch yourself to start there. If you have never given away $100 then challenge yourself to that level. If you have never given away $500 in a single donation, then take that challenge on. We should posture ourselves to give. Live to give, not to get. Success is not how much you get, but how much you give. Can you continue to challenge yourself to give larger one-time amounts?

Live a lifestyle of giving

You will orient yourself as a giver or a getter in life. It comes down to this. You will find yourself on one side or the other. They are mutually exclusive. As you walk through life, are you looking for what you can get or what you can give? Tip your waitress at the restaurant generously; look for a reason to leave a generous tip and be a blessing, not a reason to give a small one. Give to those who serve you. Quickly give your forgiveness to those who have wronged you. Give to your enemies.

> But love your enemies, do good to them, and lend
> to them without expecting to get anything back. Then
> your reward will be great (Luke 6:35).

I have found, at times, the Lord has directed me to give gifts, most often anonymously, to people I have struggled with in relationships. It has generally brought freedom into the relationship.

Give cheerfully

I have heard strained attempts to motivate people to give to finance missions and outreaches where the speaker cited how much money people spend on dog food in America. These kind of financial pleas typically leave me with an uncomfortable feeling in my stomach. Manipulated guilt is a bad motivator. It may work in the short-term, but what is gained financially in the short-term is more than offset by the bad feelings it leaves and how it closes hearts toward giving in the long-term. Prosperous people find this to be a bad motivator because their financial experience has taught them that they shouldn't make emotionally based financial decisions. Giving by compulsion or manipulation is an emotionally based decision.

Why does manipulation close the potential giver's heart? Because the scripture teaches us that God loves a cheerful giver. Why does God love a cheerful giver? When we give cheerfully, we are imitating him. We are functioning in his image as we were created to do. Do not give by compulsion, and please do not ask others to give by compulsion.

Give to those who steal from you

A few years ago, I was traveling on a trip and teaching in a pastor's training school in Africa. While we were shopping in a street market, I had some money pick-pocketed from me. At first I felt a real violation and separation from the people of this country. How dare they steal from me when I had come all this distance at my own expense to help them? However, I soon realized that for me to do any effective teaching there, I needed to "give the money away" and release the person from my judgments. Giving the money away immediately alleviated the separation and alienation I was feeling after being robbed, and reconnected me to the precious African people to whom I was attempting to minister.

Sometimes you are taken advantage of by those who literally choose to steal money or time from you. Even though something was taken, you can still "give it" to the individuals that are now in possession of your property. By doing so, you can remove the pain from the situation and actually be a cheerful giver, which releases blessing in your life. You are forgiving the person who stole from you, even though this does not mean they shouldn't be punished for what they did. I learned long ago that forgiveness does not mean the other person was right.

Give first

The farmer does not wait until he is hungry to plant the seed. He sows it early and regularly so his harvest is there when it is needed. It is important to understand that a farmer would not usually eat his seed because he knows it has more value if it is planted. "I do not have anything to give," was what the widow told Elijah. But he told her the key to her provision was to first sow a seed of what she had.

> "As surely as the Lord your God lives," she replied, "I do not have any bread—only a handful of flour in a jar and a little oil in a jug. I am gathering a few sticks to take home and make a meal for myself and my son, that we may eat it and die." Elijah said to her, "Do not be afraid. Go home and do as you have said. But first make a small cake of bread for me from what you have and bring it to me, and then make something for yourself and your son. For this is what the Lord, the God of Israel, says: 'The jar of flour will not be used up and the jug of oil will not run dry until the day the Lord gives rain on the land.'" (1 Kings 17:12–14).

This precious widow followed Elijah's instruction to give first, and then God provided a steady stream of provision for her and her family. Many of us are like this widow, she did not even realize she had a seed to sow until Elijah pointed it out. So give first. We will discuss the biblical principle of first fruits offerings in the next chapter.

Give expectantly

We have lived in a farming community for most of our lives, so we have been able to watch what farmers do. I do not know of a single farmer that plants corn and does not expect to harvest corn. No, they start planning for the harvest during the winter, long before they even plant the seed. I would dare to say that any farmer who planted seed but did not expect to harvest it would be the laughing stock of his peers. This is a biblical principle to expect to receive a return from the Lord when we plant our seed. Givers are blessed in this way.

> A generous man will himself be blessed, for he shares his food with the poor (Proverbs 22:9).

When my wife and I were first married, we were living in an apartment building. Like many young couples we were starting to save for the down-payment to purchase a house. We were just starting to put money away, and we realized we had a long way to go. We felt like we should take a seed and sow it. Since seeds reproduce after their own kind and our goal was to own a house, we wanted to give the money toward a building project of some kind. So we gave five-hundred dollars from our meager savings to help build an orphanage in Brazil. Sure enough, a few years later, we moved into a new home that we had designed and built. God brought the right people into our lives at the right time to help with the construction and purchase of the home.

If you struggle with giving and expecting a return, I respectfully encourage you to take another look at the scriptures. Luke 6:38 states clearly:

> "Give, and it will be given to you. A good measure, pressed down, shaken together and running over, will be poured into your lap. For with the measure you use, it will be measured to you."

How can this scripture be read to mean something other than what it explicitly says? Please let the truth of this scripture impact you and let it replace your feelings of false humility or wrong teaching you might have received. No, God is not a slot machine that you put something in and get something out. On the contrary he is a loving Father who has made a commitment to you which he desires to uphold. This is God's desire and his promise to us. If we learn his economy, our finances will be blessed.

Small Group Study Questions

1. How does our money represent our actions and our lives?

2. What does inflow and outflow represent?

3. Why should we give our best?

4. Why should we give more than we have before?

5. Why should we give cheerfully?

Chapter 11

Giving Defeats Materialism

My one son played on many soccer teams. I was just like every other parent out there screaming and cheering him on. I encouraged him to play his best, stay humble and be successful. I did not tell him to "do well, but not too well." I never told him to "score goals, but not too many goals." No, I cheered him on to do his best and be successful on the soccer field. I use this example to introduce the topic of balance in this teaching of biblical prosperity. Sometimes as I am teaching, people ask me what the balance is to understanding biblical prosperity. The balance to prosperity is not poverty. Biblically, there is no such thing as a little bit of prosperity and a little bit of poverty to balance it out. Giving is the action that keeps prosperity in balance.

Giving is the balance

Giving will keep money from becoming an idol in our lives. The balance to prosperity is giving. Currency has in it the word "current," which means it should keep moving like a river current. A little paradox is pointed out by the following funny story.

Picture a businessman talking to a bum on the beach about the importance of hard work. He says, "If you work hard you will be able to sit on the beach and do nothing." Of course this was what the bum was already doing. It is not about accumulating wealth to prop up our feet and relax. God wants us to be active in financing and developing his kingdom.

Many advisers on finance talk about getting rich so that you can retire early. In some cases a big fanfare is made of having a retirement party at an early age. I couldn't disagree more. This is the exact opposite of why I believe God wants to bless us. He wants to bless us so we can sow the finances we have received and empower others.

Giving defeats materialism

Giving has the power to break the back of materialism. As long as we teach, exhort and practice giving, the nasty hands of materialism will never be able to grasp us in their clutches. I cannot emphasize this enough. As we hold money openhandedly and maintain a practice of liberal giving, we have an insurance policy against materialism and the love of money. If we try to hold on to money, it will ensnare us; but if we hold it loosely, money will never control us. We will control it! Having money will never bring joy, but giving money can bring great joy.

The scriptures teach in 1 Timothy 6:10 that the love of money is the root of all kinds of evil. The "love of money" is a term that refers to materialism. Please note, this scripture does not say money is the root of all kinds of evil. If this were true, many of the Bible heroes would have been disqualified because they had abundant financial resources.

In verse 17 of this same chapter Paul explains further; "Command those who are rich in this present world not to be arrogant nor put their hope in wealth, which is so uncertain, but to put their hope in God, who richly provides us with everything for our enjoyment." Here in this verse is found another illuminating definition of materialism: putting our hope in wealth. Instead, our hope must remain in God, who gives us abundant provision for our enjoyment and for the completion of our mission. He really loves us that much!

The fear of materialism

Materialism is attempting to meet emotional or spiritual needs with material things. This is a hopeless pursuit. Material things will never satisfy the hunger of the soul. Money or material things are simply tools that the Father has given to accomplish our mission. Money must be viewed and used as a tool for his purposes versus a tool for accumulating possessions.

For years much of the church has been living in the fear of materialism—that is, a fear that if God blesses us financially, it will somehow ruin us and cause us to fall away from Him. This view ignores the many great leaders of the Bible who experienced abundance and continued steadfast in their love for the Father. There is a long list, including Abraham, Isaac, Jacob, Joseph, Noah, Job, Daniel, Jesus and Paul

Job maintained godly character when he was wealthy, when he was destitute and when his wealth was restored again. Job was the same person no matter what his financial state. He maintained his integrity and refused to deny God (Job 27:5-6). If we believe the Lord is strong enough to keep us from lust, gossip and other sins of which we are tempted within our Christian lives, why is it that we are unable to believe he is strong enough to keep us from materialism? Is materialism too big or too difficult for him to handle? Of course not!

A good friend of ours is a landlord. As sometimes happens, one of his tenants was late with the rent during the Christmas season of the year. My friend was stopping by the rental unit to collect his rent. As he was on his way, he felt prompted by the Holy Spirit to stop and buy a Christmas gift for the tenant who owed him money. So he did as he was prompted. When he visited the renter, he found her still unable to pay the money that was owed, but he still gave her the Christmas gift.

As he pondered the situation afterward, he found the Lord was showing him an example of how God loved him first even when he had a debt to pay for his sin. Yet in spite of his inability to pay for his sin himself, God still gave him the gift of eternal life by sending his son Jesus. Though he still expected the renter to pay what was owed, his obedience to give a gift led to a marvelous revelation of God's love. He has found God's hand is on the rental property business as well, and it is prospering.

Money can buy happiness if you give it away!

A recent article in Forbes magazine (September 12, 2010) by Michael I. Norton was titled, Y*es, Money Can Buy Happiness If You Give It Away*. He and his colleagues developed a very complex formula to find out how much money it would take to make people happy. They found that once people reached a certain income level, additional money did not make people happy unless they started to give it away. They concluded that accumulating material goods does not make people happy, but what really makes people happy is building relationships with others. For example, think of the wealthy person who buys multiple homes with numerous bedrooms but does not have any family and friends to host there. This is not fulfilling.

To test this idea, they approached strangers on the street and gave them different sums of money to spend. Half were told to spend it on themselves and half were told to spend it on others. Those who spent the money on themselves bought things like coffee and food, but those who spent the money on others bought gifts for family members or gave the money to the homeless. Those who spent the money on others reported feeling much happier at the end of the day than those who spent the money on themselves. It did not matter if the amount of money was large or small, it had the same result. It is not how much you spend but how you spend it that boosts the spirits.[1]

Giving firstfruits

We briefly mentioned in the last chapter the importance of giving first. Now let's take a closer look at what the Bible teaches us about firstfruits giving. A lot of people, including myself in the past, confuse the tithe with firstfruits offerings. So what is the distinction between them? The tithe is what we bring after our harvest while a firstfruits offering is what we bring before our harvest. A close examination of the scripture finds firstfruits is always mentioned before the tithe in order of giving. Succinctly stated, by honoring the Lord with the first and the best the whole or the rest is blessed.

The following scriptures refer to firstfruits giving:

> Honor the Lord with your possessions. And with
> the firstfruits of all your increase. So your barns will
> be filled with plenty. And your vats will overflow with
> new wine (Proverbs 3:9–10).

> And at the same time some were appointed over
> the rooms of the storehouse for the offerings, the first
> fruits and the tithes, to gather into them from the fields
> of the cities the portions specified by the Law by the
> priests and Levites (Nehemiah 12:44–45. See also
> Nehemiah 10:35–38 and Ezekiel 44:30).

The children of Israel brought the firstfruits before the harvest was totally gathered. This honored God, and by giving of
the first fruits, it sanctified the whole harvest. The tithe is what
we bring after our harvest, while the firstfruits is what we bring
in the beginning of the harvest as a faith gift to the Lord. This is
not a legalistic duty but another opportunity to give according to
a pattern in the Word of God.

My wife and I recently had a revelation of firstfruits offerings,
so we gave a portion of the first extra check we received for the
year above our normal income. We did this in faith, but honestly,
we were surprised to see that gift multiplied with thousands of
dollars of extra income within a month. Amazing. Then we gave
a first fruits offering on this additional income as well and saw
some more unexpected cash come in. This pattern of firstfruits
giving and tangible results happened a total of three times that

first year. I have been guilty of lumping together the firstfruits offering with tithes in the past, but I will not make this mistake anymore.

Firstfruits' giving is not something we have to do but something we get to do. If we get a revelation of firstfruits' giving, I believe it will open up a whole new level of blessing to flow in our lives. We have believed in tithing for many years, but this new revelation of the firstfruits offering as something distinct and different from the tithe, has released a whole new level of blessing in our personal finances. We discovered another way to give.

Johnny Appleseed

This brings to mind a traditional American folk hero in the United States, Johnny Appleseed. Wherever he went, he sowed apple seeds. We picture him crisscrossing the East Coast of the United States in colonial times with a big bag of apple seeds over his shoulder. On his travels, he planted apple trees that would bear apples. Wherever we go, we should be sowing finances. To the one who is sowing, more seed will be given! His store of seed will increase.

A friend of mine once told me that his son worked his way through college by being a waiter at a very popular chain restaurant. He told his dad that the staff was reluctant to work on Sundays. "And why would that be?" his dad asked. "Because all the church people come in, and they are notorious for not being generous tippers," was his son's reply. What a sad reflection and testimony this example places upon the church. We can do better than that. Do not eat all your seed by spending or storing it all. Plant it. Expect it to grow and bear fruit. No successful farmer would ever eat his seed. He knows he will not have a new crop if he consumes his seed instead of planting it.

So why don't we give?

A lot of times we don't give because we are looking at the circumstances around us instead of looking at God's word. The scriptures speak to this specifically in Ecclesiastes chapter eleven.

> Whoever watches the wind will not plant; whoever looks at the clouds will not reap. As you do not know the path of the wind, or how the body is formed in a mother's womb, so you cannot understand the work of God, the Maker of all things. Sow your seed in the morning, and at evening let not your hands be idle, for you do not know which will succeed, whether this or that, or whether both will do equally well (Ecclesiastes 11:4–6).

If we are waiting until the circumstances are just right to give, we never will do it. It takes some faith to step up to the plate and give. Seriously, I have put some checks in the offering plate with my hands shaking, my body sweating and my mind going in circles. If we are pushing the limits, as we should be, there will be some fear that we will have to overcome. This is normal for steps of faith but far from comfortable. Sow seed in the morning and in the evening. Watch to see what produces fruit.

Develop a giving portfolio

Most financial advisers recommend that you develop a diverse investment portfolio, meaning you should have investments in different types of investment vehicles. Rather than having all your money in real estate, professional advisers recommend that you put a percentage in real estate, a percentage in stocks, some in bonds, some in cash and other areas to provide stability in case one area has a decline.

In this same way, I want to encourage you to develop a diverse giving portfolio. One of the most exciting things we have done is to try and give finances into different parts of the world and to different segments of people. You can target specific geographic parts of the world, some far and some near. Are urban areas represented in your portfolio? Are the poor included in some way? How about widows? What about orphans and youth?

Give to people who will do it anyway

We want to give to people who already have goals and who are pursuing those goals with or without our help. God likes and rewards initiative and personal responsibility. When we take responsibility, he can get behind it. When people take responsibility for their vision and initiatives, in like manner, we can get behind them.

When someone makes the statement, "If I had a hundred dollars, I would take my neighbor to the Billy Graham crusade," they have not taken the responsibility yet. But when they say, "I am taking my neighbor to the Billy Graham crusade. It will cost one-hundred dollars," this statement is saying something totally different, and it shows they are taking responsibility for their vision.

People who wait around and do nothing because they have no money rarely succeed or ever find the money they desire. My observation is that God does not give to people based on need. God blesses those who apply his principles and have faith.

> For everyone who has will be given more, and he
> will have an abundance. Whoever does not have, even
> what he has will be taken from him (Matthew 25:29).

Give to the people who are going to do it with or without your help. Empower what people are already doing instead of giving a handout to start something new. Get behind a project where they are already initiating. This is how God's economy of giving works.

Give wisely

I believe we need to give in ways that meet immediate needs but also create personal responsibility and ownership. Jesus himself said the poor will always be with you. There will always be needs, which many times are genuine and we should give to that need. However, look for opportunities that "teach someone to fish instead of only giving them a fish." The following is a quote from Dennis Peacocke:

> Educated people ... seem to feel good about them-
> selves when they show compassion and heap financial
> aid on the poor.... Never mind that the so-called good
> intentions usually hurt the people receiving the aid
> in the long run.... Look at what Swedish economist
> Fredrik Erixon pointed out on the effects of aid to
> Africa:
> Africa received over $400 billion in aid between
> 1970 and 2000. Yet, the evidence presented in the

study shows an inverse relationship between aid and economic growth—when aid rises, growth falls. In part, this is because aid supplants private-sector investment and undermines savings: there is also an inverse relationship between savings and aid—when aid increases, saving decreases (Business Reform Magazine, September/October 2005).

The answer is simple: Separate pure charity, which is biblical, from investment, which is also biblical. Supply essential food, shelter, and clothing and make sure that it gets only to those who really need it, and set up investment opportunities to train and employ people to acquire real skills and real jobs. Dignity is as important as care, and care that steals dignity by maintaining poverty is cruel.[2]

Honestly, this is easier to say than to do. There are some very bright minds trying to develop ways to do this. It is possible. Micro-finance loan funds are small loans that help poor individuals in developing countries create jobs for themselves. This is one example of something that has been proven to work. The truth is we need to find more ways to do this. If we do not, then people become discouraged with their giving. If they meet the need but it is still there again next month, it can lead to weariness in giving. The truth of Proverbs 19:19 resonates loudly.

> Do not rescue someone or you will need to do it again.

In conclusion, we have spent two chapters talking about giving as the core component of God's economy. This core is central to the message of biblical prosperity. Remember Abraham was blessed to be a blessing. We will now look at some very practical steps to take.

NOTES

1   Michael I. Norton, Y*es, Money Can Buy Happiness If You Give It Away* (Forbes Magazine, 2010)

2   Dennis Peacocke, (California: Strategic Christian Services, 1995). Used by permission.

Small Group Study Questions

1. What is the balance to biblical prosperity?

2. What does the statement mean "Money can buy you happiness"?

3. Describe the difference between tithing and firstfruits giving.

4. What can we learn from Johnny Appleseed?

5. What does it mean to give wisely?

Part III

Let's Get Practical

Chapter 12

What About Budgeting?

With the pound of a gavel following the final vote, we had approved a budget of more than forty million dollars. As I glanced around the room at peoples' faces, I realized how important it was for every one of those dollars to be earmarked for a certain purpose. I sat on the board of our local public school district for nine years. We passed budgets of more than forty million dollars and all the money came from tax revenue. Our community members expected us to carefully measure and plan for every cost and expenditure that was made. Why? Because it was their tax money the school district was spending to educate the children of our community.

We could not say, "We think the costs might be higher this year, but we really are not sure, so just in case we are going to raise taxes." This kind of approach would not go over well. The community members, and also myself as a board member and a taxpayer, expect every dollar to be budgeted and accounted for.

We expect government to have a budget. Every successful business has a detailed budget. We expect our churches to have a budget. You cannot borrow money from the bank without a detailed accounting for how it will be used. Jesus even had a treasurer. So why do we find it hard to discipline ourselves to live by a personal budget?

Offense and defense

Championship sports teams usually have both a good offense and a good defense. Using this analogy, let's consider your "offense" to be your income and your "defense" to be your spending. Some people do a good job with their defense through keeping a budget, but neglect to consider how to increase their income. Other people are able to see a good income come in, but cannot be disciplined to save or invest any of the money. Can something as dull and boring as a budget help us to prosper? The answer is yes.

I usually spend most of my time teaching about the offense, which is increasing the income side. However, we will spend some time on developing a good defense because I do not want to assume anything. I have heard C. Peter Wagner say, "Whatever is assumed will be ignored." I do not want budgeting to be ignored. I have lived by a budget for most of my life and know that this has helped me to prosper. If you have been encouraged by the discussion of how to have a good "offense" financially, then hopefully you can stick with me through a short discussion of how to have a good "defense."

This is the part of the book where we want to be as practical as possible. One of the things we have found about the spirit of poverty is that it leaves people feeling as if their finances are out of control. Money seems to come in and go out quickly, and there is never enough extra to do the things the person desires. A budget allows you the opportunity to take dominion over your finances. We want to approach our finances with a quiet confidence that comes from God.

We find that as we are diligent in this financial area of budgeting that God's blessing is there. What is it that keeps us from diligence to do something simple like budgeting? In most cases it is simply laziness. As stated in Proverbs, laziness is not the path to prosperity.

> Lazy hands make a man poor, but diligent hands bring wealth (Proverbs 10:4).

I heard one minister say it like this, "Where there is lack, there is slack." What did he mean? He meant that if we are experiencing lack in our personal finances, we should examine what needs to be adjusted in our finances, because our hand is slack in some area. Let me be blunt. If you are not willing to be disciplined in the area of your spending, you will not be prosperous. Budgeting is the perfect entry-level way to become disciplined in your finances. If we read the Bible, we understand that self control is one of the fruits of the Spirit and yet many believers struggle in this area. We want the Lord to teach us to prosper, so we will need to make some changes.

We need to develop self control in our spending, in order to have the discipline needed to evaluate and take advantage of the opportunities for investment the Lord brings our way. Likewise, most of us will not have the cash necessary to invest when opportunities come our way. Please consider this. We can probably all recall an opportunity to invest that we could not take advantage of because we did not have the cash to do it. Because of not controlling spending, we miss opportunities. Jesus appointed one of the disciples to be his treasurer. Why? I presume he wanted an accurate accounting of what happened to the money. Do you think he still might be interested in this?

Personal responsibility

One reason that a budget is such a powerful tool for personal finances is that a budget forces a person to take personal responsibility for the money God is sending their way. When personal responsibility is taken, it puts you in a place where God can get behind you.

Susan (name changed) had grown up in the home of a single mom with a lot of needs. Without a father in her home she became noticeably insecure and in search of male affection. As she came into her teen years, she cultivated a pattern of behavior that often went as follows: she would break up with a guy and go on a consolation shopping spree using credit cards. Eventually she became a Christian and ended up in our living room with a credit card debt of $15,000 at the age of nineteen. As we counseled her and explained how to get on a budget, the idea of controlling spending seemed like a foreign idea to her.

Her offense was good. She made good money, but her defense had a lot of holes in it. Nevertheless, Susan submitted to the idea of a budget, and within a year and a half of us meeting with her monthly for accountability, she had eliminated her entire $15,000 debt. Now she was ready to prosper, and she did. Although she did advance financially, her greatest prosperity blessing was to meet and fall in love with a guy who loved the Lord. She was able to enter into marriage debt free. The freedom and blessing she felt in walking down that aisle and starting married life financially free was an awesome treasure for her. Susan took personal responsibility for her finances, and it opened up the door for God's blessing in many areas of her life.

Simply stated, budgeting is deciding how much you will spend each year or month in advance. Do you remember how we said that prosperous people did not make emotionally based financial decisions and this is why they did not generally respond to emotional appeals to give money? If you decide in advance what you are going to spend by setting a budget, you will not make impulsive, emotionally driven purchases. Instead your purchases will be smart, faith-filled purchases.

Every business is expected to control their costs. Why? The more they minimize costs, the better the profit margin will be and the greater the reward to the owners or stockholders. So if we are able personally to budget and control our expenses, it will allow us to save, give and invest money that will make us more prosperous. There is a saying in the business world, "No margin, no mission," simply meaning that if there is no profit then there is no incentive to function as a business. Consider your personal profit to be what income you do not spend on your living expenses. This margin then goes toward your mission.

Why is it so important to know how much you are spending and where? Consider the guy who usually buys two to three dollars worth of snack food each day on his job. This does not seem like very much money, however over the course of a year, this adds up to seven hundred to eight hundred dollars. Is this wrong? Not necessarily if this is what you are planning to spend on snack food, however it is a problem if you are spending this money on impulse buying every day.

Personally, I want to know how much I gave away last year so that I can continue to challenge myself in giving. I want to know how much I spent on food to feed my family last year, so I can plan to feed them this year. I want to know how much I am spending on vehicle maintenance because this helps me decide when it is time to get a new car that takes less maintenance. I want to know how much I am spending on interest each year because interest can sometimes be the biggest killer of giving, savings and investing.

A few years ago I was teaching a financial seminar for Christians. Dave Yarnes, a businessman from Charlotte, North Carolina, was also speaking at this conference on the subject of wealth accumulation. Dave is the owner of multiple businesses and is involved in many projects helping the poor in developing nations. He stated an interesting concept about wealth accumulation. He and his wife decided the standard of living they would live at independent of how their income increased. He feels this is one reason the Lord has blessed them with considerable resources to extend the kingdom of God. This is another reason to budget and plan how much it costs you to live.

Parkinson's law

Cyril Parkinson first wrote "Parkinson's Law" in 1955 to define the nature of government bureaucracies to expand and never get smaller.[1] It could be generally stated as the following. "The demand upon a resource tends to expand to match the supply of the resource." What is helpful for our discussion about budgeting and sometimes now known as Parkinson's second law is the statement: "Expenditures rise to meet income." Simply stated, as your income rises, so will your expenditures naturally rise to distribute that income unless a budget is developed to control the spending and provide for savings and investing. Savings eliminates the feeling that your finances are out of control and brings a sense of freedom and dominion.

How to build a budget

Hopefully this is convincing you to develop a budget if you do not already have one. The best way to build a budget is to start by writing down everything you spend for a three month period. I mean everything. This will at least give you a window into what categories to set and what a yearly budget could look like. After three months of collecting data, you are ready to take your first stab at setting a budget. Now, instead of just tracking what you are spending, you decide how much you want to spend in a certain area.

Expenses and income must be calculated on a monthly basis. Some bills like your electric bill come monthly. Others, such as your trash collection, might come every three months. Your paycheck might come every two weeks. All these transactions are averaged into monthly costs to give you a basis to compare, track past expenses and project how much you want to spend in the future by budgeting. You might be above or below for a certain month; however, your expenses should be evaluated quarterly to see if they are on track.

I am not going to go into a detailed lesson on budgeting since this book will be read in numerous countries with different currencies and various costs of living. Many financial teachers have done a lot of work in this area and have done a far better job than I. There is much available on the internet or by purchasing software that helps you with budgeting; however, I do want to point out some principles that will help you.

Tithe the ten percent

This is not a thorough and complete teaching on the tithe; however, we need to see the tithe is a biblical principle found throughout the Bible, and all of the budget should be built around this ten percent. Abraham tithed to Melchizedek before the Old Testament law was in place, it was included in the law and Jesus affirmed it after he fulfilled the law. Malachi speaks of the tithe:

> Will a man rob God? Yet you rob me. But you ask, "How do we rob you?"
>
> "In tithes and offerings. You are under a curse-the whole nation of you—because you are robbing me. Bring the whole tithe into the storehouse, that there may be food in my house. Test me in this," says the Lord Almighty, "and see if I will not throw open the floodgates of heaven and pour out so much blessing that you will not have room enough for it. I will prevent pests from devouring your crops, and the vines in your fields will not cast their fruit," says the Lord Almighty. "Then all the nations will call you blessed, for yours will be a delightful land," says the Lord Almighty (Malachi 3:8–12).

I have tithed all of my Christian life, and I know that it works. The tithe is the first ten percent. Giving offerings starts after you have paid your tithe into the storehouse. I am not looking for an argument or debate. No one is forcing you to tithe. Sometimes Christians think tithing is something they are forced to do by the church. It is not. Tithing benefits the person who is doing it.

In *Winds of Change*, Rick Joyner says:

> Abraham the father of faith, paid tithes hundreds of years before the Law, which is noted in the New Testament (see Hebrews 7:8–9) because the writer of this book was reminding Christians of this. Under the New Covenant we are a part of the Melchizedek priesthood and Melchizedek received tithes. If this was not more clearly spelled out, it is only because it was so obvious that it did not need to be.[2]

Alan Vincent, a church planter and trainer from San Antonio, Texas, gives the example of someone who came to him saying, "I cannot afford to tithe and make my house payments." Alan told him to tithe in faith and if he couldn't pay his house payment, Alan would cover it. The young man started to tithe and he never came back to Alan because he couldn't make the payment. In fact, the man soon received a promotion and a new car.

Harold Eberle, a former pastor who is now a traveling teacher and author from Yakima, Washington, relates that as a local church pastor he spent four continuous weeks teaching every Sunday on the principle of tithing. He instructed everyone to write their current income inside their Bible cover. At the end of four months of tithing, 80 percent of the congregation saw an increase in their income or some kind of financial breakthrough.

Jerry Stoltzfoos is an Assembly of God church planter and senior pastor from Gettysburg, Pennsylvania. He has planted multiple churches. He teaches on tithing and actually guarantees that the church will pay back a person's tithe if the giver did not see a significant blessing or turn around in finances after starting to tithe. He has been doing this for many years and has not paid back any tithes to date.

Simply stated, I am recommending that the number one building block of your personal financial budget should be the ten percent tithe to God. If you get involved in God's 10 percent, he will get involved in your 90 percent.

Gene Strite is a church leader, author and businessman from Chambersburg, Pennsylvania, who takes tithing a step further. When he was a pastor, his goal was to teach everyone to tithe ten percent and save ten percent. The saving ten percent will also give people the money they need stored up for financial opportunities that come their way.

A budget represents boundaries

A budget helps establish boundaries that you want in place. You need to fulfill the financial commitments you have already made before you start to spend on new commitments. For example, you have made an agreement with the electric company when you asked them to provide electricity to your home. If you give money to a homeless person on the street when you cannot pay your electric bill, you are stealing from the electric company and breaking the commitment you made with them. This is stealing, and Christians who steal will not prosper. God cannot bless people who steal and break financial commitments they have made. Those unaware of this simple, profound truth will find it difficult to get ahead financially.

If you rent a video when you haven't paid your house rent, you are stealing from the person from whom you rent your house. If you pay your neighbor's rent when you have not paid your own, you are stealing. Also, in taking responsibility for that which is not yours, you will interfere with what God is doing in the lives of others. When we try to "save" other people, we many times teach them to be more dependent upon people like us. In fact, oftentimes the recipient ends up resenting us.

To help the poor you cannot be one of them

Boundaries are good! Take care of those inside your boundaries before giving to those outside. God will give you authority only over that for which He has given you responsibility. You have a covenant to provide for your family. You do not have primary responsibility for other children. To help the poor, the best thing you can do is not be one of them. By keeping your commitments, you can bless many children. You cannot save the world when you cannot pay your bills. It does not work that way.

Your marriage covenant

While we are discussing covenants and how they affect our finances, it is important to note that the single worst financial decision you could ever make is to break the marriage covenant with your spouse and get a divorce. This is the most important boundary to keep in place. The wisdom of Proverbs backs up this idea that violation of the marriage covenant will lead to financial ruin:

> Keep to a path far from her, do not go near the door of her house, lest you give your best strength to others and your years to one who is cruel, lest strangers feast on your wealth and your toil enrich another man's house (Proverbs 5:8–10).

Your budget should contain money set aside to nurture this most important relationship in your life. This is an investment you cannot afford not to make. In the book *The Millionaire Next Door*, data shows that most millionaires are married with an average of three children. Family is very important to them. It is a prosperous mindset to keep the agreements you make and to value your spouse, children and grandchildren.

NOTES

1 Rick Joyner, *Winds of Change* (North Carolina: MorningStar Publications, Prophetic Bulletin, 2002).
2 C. Northcote Parkinson, *Parkinson's Law and Other Studies in Administration* (New York: Buccaneer Books, 1957).

Small Group Study Questions

1. How can a budget make that much difference?

2. What is our offense and our defense as it relates to our personal finances?

3. How is budgeting taking personal responsibility?

4. Why is the tithe an important building block of a budget?

5. How does a budget represent boundaries?

Chapter 13

How to Calculate
Your Net Worth

My friend, a pastor, looked at me with wide eyes as if my skin color was green and I had just walked off a spaceship from Mars. He and I had gone for a brisk morning walk along a beautiful river in rural Canada as we were preparing for a church service. Our conversation had turned to finances, and I was sharing what I was learning about net worth. He could not understand the concept and had no idea what it meant. I patiently explained to him that calculating net worth is a valuable tool to determine and accumulate wealth.

The first two questions asked of anyone who walks into the bank for any advice or funding are as follows: What do you owe (your liabilities)? How much do you own (your assets)? The bank wants to know your equity, or in simple terms, your net worth. This is a commonly used evaluation tool in the financial world to measure your financial status, however most Christians do not think in these terms when considering their own financial situation. If this is how bankers and wealthy people measure wealth, maybe we should take a look at it. It states in Proverbs that our house contains great wealth and stores of choice food, so maybe we should learn how to measure it.

> The house of the righteous contains great treasure,
> but the income of the wicked brings them trouble
> (Proverbs 15:6).

As I dialogued with many Christians, I found that very few even understood the concept of net worth. When you hear the term millionaire, you are hearing about a person who has a net worth of more than a million dollars. Please understand, I am not saying everyone should be a millionaire, I am only asking you to think like a millionaire. The point here is to change our thinking to a more prosperous manner of thinking. This is why I am challenging you to calculate your net worth.

The truth is, as we calculate our net worth, it might even result in a negative number. This is not a cause for alarm. It is reality. It does not matter as long as we see this as a starting point and believe to increase this number. The issue is not how much you own, it is how you think about what you own. You are a manager of what God has given you. Determine your net worth and make a plan to increase it. In discussing net worth, I want to be clear that financial net worth in no way minimizes the fact that we are all of great worth to the Lord Jesus. We are of worth to him because we are created in his image and he loves us. Understanding our financial net worth will help us fulfill our destiny.

Determine your net worth

This is a simple matter of listing all of your assets and how much they are currently worth after subtracting what you owe on them. Part of the process is to determine how much equity you have in your house if you own it. To do this you determine the fair market value of your house and subtract the amount you owe on it in a mortgage. You do the same for your furniture, your cars, everything you own. You might have some retirement funds. These are added to the asset side of your net worth. If you have debt, like credit cards, this is subtracted on the liability side. When you add all the assets together and subtract all the liabilities this gives you your net worth. I have included a simple worksheet in Appendix F for you to do it. If you do not do it now, do it when you finish this chapter. It will take time and some research to complete it. You can download an electronic copy of this worksheet which automatically calculates the results at www.h2hp.com/products/a-practical-path-to-a-prosperous-life.

Remember, if the net worth you determine is small or even negative, this is not a problem because you are changing your thinking. When I first started to calculate my net worth, I did it every six months. It was amazing to watch it grow little by little. This was really encouraging. In the midst of a busy life of paying bills for kids in sports, birthdays, buying food and clothes, and so forth, it really did not "feel" like we were getting ahead. But I would calculate my net worth halfway through the year, and sure enough, it was increasing because of some decisions we had made at the beginning of the year.

I started to set goals for the amount I wanted my net worth to grow each year. Sometimes I made the goals, but even if I did not, my net worth still increased. Now, I just calculate it every year instead of every six months. Occasionally, the Lord would bring a significant opportunity my way and my net worth would jump substantially in one year. I learned that he can do more in a year than I could do in five years.

In the book *The Millionaire Next Door*[1], the authors state that most millionaires have not inherited a large amount of money, but are wealthy as a result of having a good offense and a good defense. The information given shows that most millionaires are still making somewhere in the range of $100,000, but are able to save/invest twenty thousand per year to develop their net worth.

The four commonly agreed upon factors that help increase net worth are increasing income, increasing savings, decreasing expenditures (via budgeting) and reducing your debts. To be wealthy you really do not need a bigger house, you need a bigger net worth, although sometimes the two are related. Because wealthy people think in terms of net worth, they balance their spending on enjoyment with investing for financial freedom tomorrow.

Think of family wealth

The powerful thing about calculating net worth is that it moves you away from thinking about hourly wages and your next raise to thinking in terms of assets and liabilities. Do not think in terms of an hourly wage, this is limiting and disappointing. If you are thinking in terms of your next hourly raise, this can only happen at the end of the year or at an annual review. When it does, you will find that generally as wages increase so do your taxes. Hand-to-mouth living is not God's will. Think in terms of your net worth. This is essential to prosperity.

We learn from the Bible that a portion of what you accumulate should be a blessing to your children. An inheritance consciousness helps you think and act prosperously today. It causes you to think of increasing net worth on a long-term basis.

> A good man leaves an inheritance for his children's children, but a sinner's wealth is stored up for the righteous. Houses and wealth are inherited from parents, but a prudent wife is from the Lord (Proverbs 19:14; 13:22).
> ... You still the hunger of those you cherish; their sons have plenty, and they store up wealth for their children (Psalm 17:14).

Do not just live to meet your needs. This is selfish. Why would we live and believe for merely enough to meet our needs, when we have the capacity in God to believe for more, meet the needs of others and pass the balance on to our children?

Studies have continually shown that small businesses create more than 70 percent of the new jobs in America, and most of these are family run businesses.[2] The most powerful drive to succeed is family, and family is held together by faith. This is the basic infrastructure that has sustained America's prosperity and growth. If you think about it, most of the largest corporations in the world started out as family-owned small businesses. A portion of what you accumulate is meant to be a blessing to your children. When you receive an inheritance from your parents, you are receiving the fruits of their labors. It represents their time, their passions, their labor and wisdom passed on to you.

An olive tree is a picture of a generational blessing passed on to the next generation. The Psalmist said, "I am like an olive tree flourishing in the house of God; I trust in God's unfailing love forever and ever." When a Hebrew farmer planted an olive tree, he would be planting it for his children. If we are to flourish like an olive tree, we need to start thinking in a long-term framework. The leaves of an olive tree were considered to signify abundance. Many times an olive tree lived for 500 years.

Train your children to be givers. Let them see you be generous with others. Teach them God's economy. This applies to both your spiritual children and your natural children. To train means teaching them the information, demonstrating for them to observe and see, giving them the chance to do it and coaching them afterwards. Most will learn your financial values and be good stewards of what you pass on to them.

What should my net worth be?

In his book, *Becoming a Millionaire God's Way*, Dr. C. Thomas Anderson gives the following formula to determine if you are on track with growing your net worth. I found this to be helpful, and you might find that you are not even that far off track for your season of life. Remember: do not expect to get rich quick, this is a life-long goal. Advancement comes to those who diligently apply God's principles on a consistent, long-term basis.

> Now determine what your net worth should be at this time of your life. Take your taxable income for the last year and multiply it by your age. (If computing these numbers for a husband and wife together, use either person's age but you will be better off using the older one). Divide that number by ten and you will have the amount your net worth should be at this point

in your life. By subtracting your actual net worth you can see how far off you are.[3]

Complete this calculation. It really works and gives you a practical place to begin to take steps forward.

Thinking in terms of net worth

Now, take a moment and let the impact of this thinking settle into your heart. At issue is not your net worth but thinking in terms of net worth and increasing it. Start now. Make a plan to increase your net worth. We will talk more about this in the next chapter. Saving and investing 5 percent to 10 percent of your income would be a good place to start in a long-term financial plan. However, the most important part is that you start doing something.

One truth of God's economy of giving that I did not cover in chapters 10 and 11 is this: Do not give it all away. Yes, you read correctly. For many years I have thought and stated publicly the opposite of this—that if I was given a sum of money; the most spiritual thing to do would be to give it all away. I have changed my mind. If given a sum of money now I would certainly give some of it away, but as the following scripture indicates I would also save and invest a significant portion of it so that my net worth increases. As my net worth increases I can give more away each year for many years.

In the house of the wise are stores of choice food and oil, but a foolish man devours all he has (Proverbs 21:20).

Think about it. A farmer does not usually eat his seed. He plants it. He does not eat his laying hen or milking cow. No, he nurtures and feeds them so that they produce daily. They produce regularly for a long time. This is what a high net worth can do for you. It will give you the opportunity to give regularly for a long period of time. We want to give abundantly year after year. So let's plan to do so.

NOTES

1   Thomas J. Stanley, *The Millionaire Next Door* (New York: Pocket, 1996).
2   Data from the Small Business Administration and the Bureau of Labor Statistics show this is true when talking about the new jobs created in the private sector, which provides the majority of the jobs in the U.S.
3   Dr. C. Thomas Anderson, *Becoming a Millionaire God's Way* (New York: Faith Words, Hachette Book Group, 2006), p.2.

Small Group Study Questions

1.   Explain how you calculate net worth.

2.   Why is it important to calculate net worth?

3.   Why is it important to think about family wealth?

4.   What does it mean to think like a farmer?

5.   Why does it not matter if your net worth is negative?

Chapter 14

Jacob Had a Financial Plan

William Munyanya is in an African entrepreneur who lives in the Kitale region of Kenya. He told me the story of trying to teach some of his neighbors to think more prosperously by thinking long term instead of short term. Kitale is a rich agricultural area of Kenya and its biggest cash crop is corn, which they call maize. The problem with selling the maize they harvest is that it is all harvested at the same time, and this creates a glut on the local market and drives the price of the corn down.

William explained to his neighbors that they could put their maize in storage for six months and then get twice the price for it. Of course it would cost them some money for storage, but they would still make significantly more than if they sell it at harvest time. William was ready to hire the storage space so they could all share that cost together. As he finished his proposal, his neighbors' response was to laugh at him. In their minds, they had never heard of such a stupid thing. They did not believe him because they were so used to getting all the cash right away at harvest. It did not matter to them that if they waited, they would actually get more cash, almost twice as much. They could not see it. There focus was only on today's need. William ended up doing it himself to prove it to them. He wanted to demonstrate for them that long-term thinking is more prosperous thinking than just thinking for today.

Another example of this kind of long-term thinking is how William is preparing to get electricity to his house. He built a house in a rural area that has no access to electricity. In rural Africa, electricity is not available along every road but only where people pay to have it installed. William's family knew when they built the house that the closest electricity was located miles away, and they do not have the money to pay for it to get there.

William researched what type of tree the electric company uses for electric poles, and he has planted a stand of this kind of trees on his property. These tall slender trees grow fairly rapidly, however, it will still take seven to eight years for them to be large enough for him to trade or sell to the electric company for electrical service. It will take time, but he will get electricity to his home for his family.

Think long range

Prosperous people think and act with long-range goals in mind. Today's labor may not pay off for years. Job was a man who learned to look at the long-term picture. He lived one-hundred-forty years in God's blessing after the devastation he experienced. We will be more prosperous today by thinking about paying next year's bills. The mind set on the long term produces patience today. Poverty thinking focuses on today's need.

In our rental property business, we learned it was to our

benefit to think long term. When we first started, we did not take adequate time to screen the renters to make sure they had a history of paying their bills and had a desire and the resources to stay in the apartment for a long time. Instead, we quickly tried to fill the vacancies so we would not miss one month's rent. We learned the hard way that quickly filling the vacancies caused a lot of turnover and each time there was a change, it cost us extra money in advertising, maintenance and sometimes legal fees. We learned that it was fiscally better for us to take a long-term approach to the rental business and find long-term renters.

A prosperous man buys good tools and takes care of them, because he wants to use them all his life and pass them on to his sons. A prosperous mindset will cause you to be a good steward of the things the Lord has given to you. You will want to take care of them so that they last a long time. Many times in poor countries you can see vehicles overloaded way beyond capacity in order to reach an immediate destination. The drivers do not give any thought to taking care of the vehicles in order for the vehicles to last for long-term use.

When we start to think long range, it changes the way we approach life. It changes the way we buy things. When my wife and I saw this principle, we stopped buying a bunch of cheap, plastic toys for our kids and started to buy better quality toys that our kids could use and that should last for our grandkids to use.

A business person is often thinking five to ten years down the road. I spoke with one individual in the United States who had built a significant number of chicken houses on a farm. He and his partners will be using the proceeds to pay off their capital investment in the construction for the first nine to ten years of operation. However, after ten years, the construction cost will be paid and the chicken houses will turn into a highly profitable and lucrative investment. You need to be able to see ten years down the road to get there.

In conversation with another business man who had started multiple businesses, I learned another application of thinking long term. He stated that when he was first starting a business, he never kept track of the amount of hours he put into it because it would not make sense to put that many hours into a business with the minimal initial return. The return came years later, after the business got off the ground and started to generate returns on a larger scale. This insight helped me when we started the property rental business that required a lot of initial start-up work in the first few years.

Thinking long term causes us to step back and take more of an overview of our lives, careers and families. For example a church leader might want the church to grow and be a blessing to the people who get involved. This is a good and godly thing to desire. However the church leader should not think in terms of trying to invite one new person to the church. He should be thinking bigger by creating a spiritually enriching environment that will draw many new people to the church.

Think for example of the advertisements for soft drinks. The advertisements never specifically say, "Go to the store and buy a Coke." No, the advertisements show the fun things of life and portray the soft drink as a part of that. The key is that beverage owners do not want you to buy one soft drink, they want you to buy their soft drink for a lifetime. This is thinking long term in their marketing.

Great restaurants do not sell individual meals, they create an atmosphere. An effective insurance salesman does not look to sell you a single insurance policy. He wants to develop a relationship with you, because he wants your business for a lifetime.

Thinking long term changed how I buy tires

My tutoring from the Holy Spirit continued. I was having a conversation with a gentleman I met, and we started to talk about cars. He commented about a certain vehicle that he had owned and what a good truck it was. He said he had bought it new and owned it until it had 120,000 miles on it. This was a new concept to me since I had never purchased a new car, but his next comment really got my attention. He said he had gone through two sets of tires in the life of the vehicle. I thought he was joking. "What do you mean two sets of tires?" I asked. He replied it had a good set of tires when he purchased the vehicle and the tires lasted for sixty-thousand miles. He replaced the old tires by purchasing an expensive set of tires that lasted for the second sixty-thousand miles.

I was amazed. I started to think about what happened when I went to buy tires. I would walk into the tire store and scan the racks of tires until I found the least expensive ones, purchase them and leave thinking about what a bother it was to spend money and time buying tires. Unfortunately the reality was that the cheap tires soon wore out and before I knew it, I was back in the tire store scanning the racks for the cheapest tires once again. I did not realize it at the time, but the spirit of poverty was affecting the way I bought tires. I was just thinking about saving a few dollars in the short term and not thinking about the long-term effect. We owned two vehicles, and between the two of them, I was spending a lot of time and energy at the tire store.

A better quality of life

I contrasted my experience with this man's experience. Somehow, what he was describing seemed like a better path to take. It seemed like a more prosperous path. I changed my method of tire purchasing and started to buy better tires that lasted longer. I spent a lot less of my time and energy shopping for tires and had more of both for important things like my family. The more expensive tires gave my cars a smoother ride, and my family felt safer in bad weather. My new tire-buying strategies gave me a better quality of life. I found a better way, a more prosperous way.

There might be times when it is appropriate to buy inexpensive tires for a vehicle; however, in my personal life, this was one area where the Lord was specifically working to uproot a spirit of poverty in my life.

Developing a financial plan

Developing a financial plan might seem very carnal and unspiritual. Some of us might even react to it because there are many people who are not Christians who are making financial plans. However, we must realize there are times that the Lord asks us to do things that look a lot like the things the rest of the world is doing.

A case in point is the Old Testament sacrifices that were required of the children of Israel. Though they were unique in some ways and done in the name of Jehovah, the truth is that to the objective observer they were a bloody mess that looked a lot like many of the pagan rituals practiced in that day.

We must be secure enough to do what the Lord is asking us to do. It could be radically different—like spitting in someone's eye to heal them. Or, it could look like what everyone else is doing—Jesus getting baptized in the Jordan with many others.

A closer examination of the scriptures shows us that many in the Bible had a financial plan. Joseph had a plan. Jacob had a plan. Poverty-minded people have a difficult time setting goals or verbalizing their plans for the future. Can we move in the opposite spirit of this? Yes, we should live like the Lord Jesus might return tomorrow, but we should plan like he will not return for forty years.

When we write a financial plan, it forces us into the discipline of thinking long term instead of short term. Planning can be one of our greatest skills. Many Christians think that planning is contrary to God's nature; however nothing could be further from the truth. In Isaiah, we find the Lord talking about his plan.

> … What I have said, that will I bring about; what I
> have planned, that will I do (Isaiah 46:11).

Is God's plan completely scripted and unchangeable? I do not think so. I believe his plan has some variables built into it. It has to because he is working with us. But it is still a plan. The scriptures state that the plans of the diligent lead to prosperity:

> The plans of the diligent lead to profit as surely as
> haste leads to poverty (Proverbs 21:5).

Start by dreaming with God

We have already learned from Deuteronomy 8:18 that it is the Lord who gives us the ability to produce wealth. The author of creativity is in you. Do not think small. God is not small. Remember, thinking about getting a second or third job is the wrong idea! This is short-term, poverty thinking. Do not just work harder and become a workaholic. Find a way to have your money work hard for you.

> Do not wear yourself out to get rich; have the wisdom to show restraint (Proverbs 23:4).

Change your thinking. Lift up your eyes. Get off the tricycle and on a bicycle or in a car. Create wealth. Help people succeed. Move from earning money to seed planting and creating wealth. Think of new ideas that help people. The person who takes time to solve other people's problems is opening the door for his or her own advancement. Your ability to create never will be greater than your concept of God, as Frank Schaeffer indicates: Prosperity comes from creative ideas that create wealth and enhance culture.[1] Let us carefully read what Jacob used for his financial plan. It is very detailed and very specific. He planned it carefully and followed his plan and became prosperous.

> "… let me go through all your flocks today and remove from them every speckled or spotted sheep, every dark-colored lamb and every spotted or speckled goat. They will be my wages. And my honesty will testify for me in the future, whenever you check on the wages you have paid me. Any goat in my posses-

sion that is not speckled or spotted, or any lamb that is not dark-colored, will be considered stolen. Jacob … took fresh-cut branches from poplar, almond and plane trees and made white stripes on them by peeling the bark and exposing the white inner wood of the branches. Then he placed the peeled branches in all the watering troughs, so that they would be directly in front of the flocks when they came to drink. When the flocks were in heat and came to drink, they mated in front of the branches. And they bore young that were streaked or speckled or spotted. Jacob set apart the young of the flock by themselves, but made the rest face the streaked and dark-colored animals that belonged to Laban.… Whenever the stronger females were in heat, Jacob would place the branches in the troughs in front of the animals so they would mate near the branches, but if the animals were weak, he would not place them there. So the weak animals went to Laban and the strong ones to Jacob. In this way the man grew exceedingly prosperous and came to own large flocks, and maidservants and menservants, and camels and donkeys (Genesis 30:29–43).

So where did Jacob come up with this detailed financial plan? The scriptures did not specifically tell us, but it would seem like he got it from spending time with God. I love the fact that Jacob's financial plan was part natural and part supernatural. Norm Schlemmer is a church leader and a businessman from Indiana. Here he describes how he gets ideas from God.

Ask God to give you ideas for continuous streams of income. One example I had was when I asked God how I would pay for college educations for my four children. After I bought my first apartments, the Holy Spirit told me to buy ten sets of coin-operated washers and dryers and put them in the apartments. I paid for the laundry appliances the first year and have now had them for more than twenty years. It was very little work, other than hauling the quarters to the bank. The profits from the washers paid for my children's college and then some. The washers are still producing today with almost no involvement. Being obedient to the Holy Spirit can have great rewards.

If a farmer plants corn in the spring, he harvests the crop in the fall. If he plants apple seeds in the spring, it may be many years before he can reap. The difference between the corn and the apple tree is that the corn is harvested only once and has to be replanted the next year. The apple tree will yield many years of harvest from one planting. Buying stock in a company can yield many years of dividends. Ask God to show you long-term investments.[2]

Norm makes it sound easy, and it does get easier as you go; however, let me be honest. It will be difficult as you sit with a pencil in your hand or in front of a keyboard asking God to get you started on a financial plan. Difficult, but not impossible. Do not give up. Push through until you have something written. Your financial plan to increase your net worth will help you to focus your time and energy in a specific direction and be effective.

A written financial plan

It takes time to write out a financial plan, because it forces you to think through the process. God told Habakkuk to write the revelation down and make it plain so that a herald could run with it. If you never have written a financial plan, you probably will struggle to get it done. You start to save 3 to 5 percent of your income by budgeting—what do you do with it? Faith has to precede the financial blessing of God or you do not know if it is from God. You have to ask God to help, and you have to ask others for help.

> Commit to the Lord whatever you do, and your plans will succeed. Plans fail for lack of counsel, but with many advisers they succeed (Proverbs 16:3–4; 15:22).

What if my financial plan does not work?

My experience is that financial plans seldom work out exactly as written and that they need to be re-written every few years. Here is what Rick Joyner says about planning.

> Nothing of lasting significance has ever been accomplished without some type of planning or preparation. Every general goes into battle with a battle plan and every coach goes into a game with a game plan.[2]

When a sports team is preparing for competition the coach develops and the athletes focus on a game plan and practice relentlessly to execute it. At the same time the coach and the players make decisive changes at halftime or mid game as needed to get the victory. Likewise Marines are taught plans and maneuvers and go into every battle with a battle plan. They are told no battle will ever go as planned and that adjustments will need to be made along the way. A financial plan will seldom work out exactly as planned, but will get you far enough to know what corrections or adjustments are needed for success.

Does the fact that the game plan might change at halftime keep a team from developing a game plan? No. Does the fact that the battle plan will likely change during the battle keep the Marines from developing a battle plan? Of course not. They plan to win but are ready for anything that might come their way. Sometimes you win and sometimes you learn. Failure will only make you stronger and smarter.

Think like a farmer

Everyone knows that a farmer works hard physically. But a farmer has his crops growing while he is sleeping. If it is raining during the night his crops are being watered while he sleeps. Many investments work this way. Think of your dollars invested as working for you as you are sleeping. There is something inherently good about this. It is called passive income because you do not have to do anything for it to yield increase as opposed to active income that is payment for your labor.

Plant a seed and several months later that seed will produce fruit with dozens of seeds. Investing is one way of planting seeds for the future. Plant now, the harvest is in the future. The average stock related investment doubles every seven years. These are not chance deals with big risk. Begin to live on the harvest and not the seeds. Do not eat your seed. Make a goal to save and invest

10 percent of your income. It's okay to start with 2 or 3 percent and work up to 10 percent.

Consider the story Jesus told about the talents (Matthew 25: 14-30). Jesus was literally talking about investing money. Spiritual gifts (what we sometimes call talents) are a secondary application of these scriptures. As we will discuss later, a talent in Jesus' day was a set amount of money. Think in terms of planting seeds, time to grow and reaping. This biblical principle is called seed time and harvest. It is found throughout the Bible.

Some people are waiting around for God to do a financial miracle. Their faith might be fixed on Proverbs 13:22, "And the wealth of the sinner is stored up for the righteous." If those Christians simply applied the principles in God's word, the wealth of the sinners would begin to flow into their hands. Instead, they are waiting for God to fulfill his word, but he is waiting for them to apply his principles and plant some seeds.

The financial plan

Consider a financial plan for youself. It is very important to remember you are not competing against anyone else. This is not a race! That would be a wrong motivation. This is between you and God. I have included the actual worksheet in Appendix F for you to copy and use or it can be found at www.h2hp.com/products/a-practical-path-to-a-prosperous-life for you to download. I recommend that you prayerfully complete this after you have finished the book.

You will use your regular net worth calculation to monitor the success of your financial plan. Just do it. Get started. The longer you wait, the harder it will be to start. Do not slip into the delusion that you will get rich overnight. Instead, plan to move into a prosperous lifestyle gradually.

NOTES

1   Norm Schlemmer *From the Top* (blog, 2011).
2   Rick Joyner, *Prophetic Bulletin* (North Carolina: MorningStar, 2008).

Small Group Study Questions

1. Explain why thinking long range is a more prosperous way of thinking than short term.

2. Why don't you ever see a commercial telling you to buy a coke?

3. Research and describe Joseph's financial plan.

4. Describe Jacob's financial plan.

5. Why is it important to write down your financial plan?

Chapter 15

Let's Get
Brutally Honest

From history we know that when William Bradford founded the first English colony in America in Jamestown, Virginia, the first couple of years were very tough for the new colony. One reason was because they had a community garden in which all were to labor. It ended up that only a few demonstrated the incentive to do the work, and many people died in the first year. After a couple of years, they decided to split the garden into plots and give each family a plot of ground from which they were to work and eat. From that point on, there was plenty of food in Jamestown. Individuals took personal responsibility for their own provisions. That made a big difference and the settlement at Jamestown survived.

To apply this principle, shall we sit around and fantasize about how much we would like to give or shall we start to work the land in order to gain an abundance to give? Proverbs 28:19 states, "He who works his land will have abundant food, but the one who chases fantasies will have his fill of poverty." We cannot give what we do not have, so let's quit being spiritually lazy and start believing God for abundance. How can we make our soul prosperous? Unless we change some of our thoughts and actions, we will get the same financial result that we have gotten before. We can have great intentions about building a budget, calculating net worth and developing a financial plan, but if we do not put action to it nothing will change.

Risk

A pastor friend of mine said the following after he was physically assaulted at a New Year's Eve celebration, "Christianity is all theory until it is put to the test." The pastor's ability to live out Christianity was put to a test, and he passed as he forgave the individual and moved on with life. This statement is true about our belief in biblical prosperity too. It is all theory unless it is put to the test. We started this book by looking at the blessings of Abraham. He was blessed to be a blessing. He received the blessing of God by faith. We need to do it the same way. It has often been said that faith is spelled RISK.

In the book *Good to Great*, author Jim Collins talks about how to confront the brutal facts without losing faith. Start with an honest approach to assess the given situation. Do not confuse faith that you are going to prevail with the brutal facts and reality of your current situation. The reality of your present situation, perhaps as measured by net worth, gives the sound footing needed to lift yourself out of it. We must look reality in the eye and confront it.

Confronting fear

In the wake of the September 11, 2001 terrorist bombing and destruction of the World Trade Center, many were overcome with fear and intimidation. The magnitude of physical destruction and the sense of violation shook people to the core of their being. As people responded to this tragedy differently, I heard one Christian ministry felt led of the Lord to confront the fear that was associated with it. They scheduled a meeting on the one year anniversary, right in Manhattan, to confront any intimidation or fear people were feeling in regards to this terrorist attack. This really got my attention as the right thing to do, so my son and I traveled to New York for the one-year anniversary of 9/11. It was a great night, and as you know there were no follow up attacks. It proved to be a great lesson for my son in confronting opposition and fear.

We need to face the spirit of poverty head on and confront it. If we are brutally honest, this is how we develop a prosperous soul. It will take risk and financial courage. Remember the parable of the talents? The one steward did not understand God's nature and so he did not take a risk with his talent. He was punished by the master for not taking a risk. For those of us who want to understand God's nature, we are required to take risks. Without faith, it is impossible to please God.

Let's get brutally honest

A prosperous person will be outcome-based not hourly-based. The hourly-based person will put in a lot of time and be happy with that even if the objectives have not been reached. "I did my best and tried hard. I feel good about my effort. If you want, I can tell you about how hard I tried. It is a great story." But what is the outcome? Either you put a budget together or you do not. A prosperous person will look for a way to achieve the goal. Either you will initiate change or things will stay the same. But even if you initiate steps to change some of those steps might not work. Do not be satisfied to have taken steps, persevere with needed adjustments until change occurs.

Be realistic and recognize failure to achieve desired outcomes, though this should be done in a positive environment. Failure is not the enemy of success but rather the teacher of success. This is a valuable tool. I am sure you have heard of the great number of failures Abraham Lincoln experienced before he was elected President of the United States, or of the thousands of times Edison tried the light bulb before he discovered how it worked. For some, failure defeats them, and yet for others failure motivates them.

I was recently stirred by reading about the history of Wall Street in the book *Becoming a Millionaire God's Way* by C. Thomas Anderson. What struck me was that the original folks who started to trade on Wall Street were just normal people like you and me selling war bonds. Everyone starts somewhere.

> Throughout history the wealthy got that way in the same manner that they do today. They invested. They watched for opportunities and took calculated risk based on their knowledge of how money works.
>
> Most Americans have heard of the British East India Company. It was formed in 1602 and began to buy spices, teas and other goods from the Far East. It was some of that tea that our forefathers made famous in the Boston Tea Party. That might be considered a setback, but those who invested in the company when

it started multiplied their money 143 times.

In 1789, the United States government had just emerged from the Revolutionary War and was completely broke. To raise some capital, it sold eighty million dollars of government bonds. The government desperately needed money and those who were aware could invest in the government and earn substantial dividends.

The men who sold these bonds were called broachers. The term originally referred to those who broached or tapped a keg of wine. They punched a hole in the keg so that its contents could be poured out. The government broachers were tapping the finances of people and bringing them into the government. In time the "a" was dropped and they became known as "brokers."

These broachers worked largely in the capital, which was New York at that time. To avoid inclement weather they often worked out of a place called the Turvine Café. This gathering was the beginning of what became known as the New York Stock Exchange. The café was located on a little four block street called Wall Street. When the Dutch first settled New York in 1644, they put brush wood around their complex to keep cattle and Indians out. The governor later built a nine-foot-high wall, turning the area into a fortress. The street that ran along the wall became known as Wall Street.

I mention this little bit of history because it shows that there have always been opportunities for invest-

ments and there have always been investors. There is
no reason why you cannot be one.[1]

I agree with Dr. Anderson. There is no reason why we cannot
become financially literate, develop financial courage and start
to prosper. Desire is one of God's focusing points. He uses it to
get people moving. We have read previously that God gives us
the desires of our hearts. The very fact that you have an interest
in this book and are reading it indicates that you desire to change
and learn.

Brian goes to Wall Street

I have my own story about Wall Street as well. In my mind
Wall Street was this big imposing financial mountain that was
too big for anyone normal like me to climb. I have heard many
times the comparison of Wall Street versus Main Street implying
that Wall Street (representing the financial world) is at odds with
Main Street (the normal Mom and Pop world where most of us
live). Although there is some truth to this comparison, I have come
to realize that most of what is listed and traded on Wall Street is
owned by people who live on Main Street.

So here is my Wall Street story. This is one of those times
where I felt the Lord was answering my prayer for the Holy Spirit
to teach me to prosper. In order to increase my financial literacy
I was in the habit of reading about Wall Street in the Wall Street
Journal. I realized that I was scheduled to speak at a conference
in Brooklyn, New York, which is in close proximity to Wall Street
in Manhattan. I started to get the nudge of the Holy Spirit that
I should actually go to Wall Street. I felt I should go there, pray,
listen and get a cup of coffee. After finishing the conference and

getting directions, I set out to visit Wall Street on my way home. What an adventure.

I made it across the Brooklyn Bridge only to become hopelessly lost in a myriad of multiple lane, one way streets and construction in Manhattan. I was finally able to make my way down to the south of Manhattan Island where Wall Street is located, but I still could not find it. Believe me it was a little embarrassing to stop and ask someone for directions to Wall Street in the shadows of the financial district skyscrapers —how intimidating—I almost gave up and went home. Finally I worked my way between a couple of tall buildings and saw the sign for Wall Street. How disappointing!

I was expecting it to be one of these multiple lane streets bustling with traffic and commerce. It is not. Wall Street is two lanes wide (and one of them is for parking). The section I first found is open only to pedestrians. You cannot even drive on it. I snaked my way around until I found a way to turn on to the part of it that you can drive on. This is the same Wall Street that intimidates people around the world? It is just a narrow street.

And then there it was—a parking spot! This was a miracle in and of itself. I self-consciously pulled into the spot and left my car running in case anyone asked me to move. When you are obeying God in new ventures, you look for his thumbprint there. This simply means some sign or recognition that you are on the right track. As I sat there with my car idling, I saw someone walk by with a coffee cup marked with the logo of my favorite coffee shop. I smiled. Yes! I knew I was exactly where God wanted me to be.

I took my Bible and the pages fell open to the scriptures in Genesis that speak of Abraham being the Father of many nations and when he was introduced to El Shaddai the God of more than enough. For me that day the wall of intimidation that surrounded Wall Street came down. I wrote down the things God was showing me, found the coffee shop, enjoyed a coffee and drove home. I had climbed a mountain.

Let's get started

You might recall that the spirit of poverty leaves you feeling like your finances are out of control. The money comes in and goes out without you having control of it. Here are some risky, beginner suggestions to help you practically take dominion over your finances. Consider these ideas and take some action as the Lord is leading you. You should be taking action on at least three of the following fifteen items.

1. Understand the scriptural power of the tithe and do it with faith in your heart that God will pour out overflow to you.
2. Deposit your money into savings and "own it" for a while before moving it into checking to pay bills. Even if it is only for a few days, it will change your thinking and give you a sense of dominion.
3. Take dominion over your finances and pay a bill early instead of waiting until the last possible time. You take authority and decide when to pay the money.
4. Most poverty stricken people have filled their lives with second rate possessions. Buy something you do not need but can afford. It should be one nice item of lasting value like a watch

or picture for the wall. Get something that you can keep at a very visible, prominent place. Do not buy the cheapest or even the best deal, but purchase something beautiful that feeds your soul. If you need to do this to break a poverty mindset, you will find it a struggle to do. Buy something you can pay for with cash.

5. If you have never owned any stock, set aside $150 and buy a few shares of stock to own. Not every broker will do it, but some will.

6. If you have never given away one hundred dollars at one time, do it as soon as you can save it up.

7. Subscribe to a year of the Wall Street Journal. Let your soul prosper as you read.

8. Plant or expand some flower gardens around your house. Beauty feeds your soul.

9. Fix something that is broken around your property. Especially something that has been broken for a long time. Repair or replace it permanently and with good quality materials.

10. Sign up for a course at a community college or trade school. Look for something you like to do or think you would enjoy. It could be something career oriented like a marketing course or something that feeds your soul like an art course.

11. Take half of the time you are presently spending on entertainment and use if for learning. Be specific and measureable. Read an economics book instead of watching your favorite sports team.

12. Follow the instructions in chapter 13 of this book and calculate your net worth.

13. Follow Dr. Thomas Anderson's formula found in chapter 13 to measure if you are on track with growing your net worth for your age.

14. Develop a ten year financial plan that makes adjustments in all four elements of net worth: income, expenditures, savings and debt.

15. Find a quiet place and pray the prayer, "Holy Spirit, teach me to prosper."

You have heard many of my stories of how I formerly believed one way, but later realized that I was looking at the situation through the eyeglasses of the spirit of poverty, so I changed my mind to a more prosperous mindset. He is still showing me things I can change. You can do the same. If you prayed and asked the Holy Spirit to teach you to prosper, he will do it—not only through the head knowledge you gain from reading a book, but he will teach you prosperous actions to take as well.

I recently came across an old African proverb. Here is what it said, "The best time to plant a tree is twenty years ago. The second best time is now."

NOTES
1   Dr. C. Thomas Anderson, *Becoming a Millionaire God's Way*, (New York: Faith Words, Hachette Book Group, 2006).

Small Group Study Questions

1. What is a broacher?

2. Why is it significant to know how Wall Street got started?

3. Why is honesty with yourself so important in developing a prosperous soul?

4. How can failure be a good teacher?

5. How does God give you the desires of your heart?

Chapter 16

Hot Tips
for Investing

"... When the Indians sold Manhattan Island, New York City, to Peter Minuit of the Dutch West India Company for $24 in beads and trinkets, they did not get a bad deal. If they had invested that money at an 8 percent annual rate of return, that $24 would be worth $27 trillion dollars today. They could today buy Manhattan back and have plenty of money left over. The problem was not the amount of money but the lack of a plan for it."[2]
— Robert T. Kiyosaki, *Rich Dad Poor Dad*

This might surprise you but the key element in the previous scenario is not the percentage of return on investment but the amount of time over which the investment is calculated. If you are expecting God to give you some hot, new, never-thought-of-before, high-return financial investing ideas—get over it! He might give you some unique ideas eventually as you learn to apply the basic, common sense principles in this book, but for now he just wants you to start somewhere. To deaden your excitement even more let's look at another quote about investing from Robert T. Kiyosaki:

> "Many people think investing is this exciting process where there is a lot of drama. Many people think investing involves a lot of risk, luck, timing and hot tips. ... to me investing is a plan, often dull, boring and almost mechanical process."

For most of us it will likely start with the difficult discipline of saving some money so we have something to invest. Not only will it be dull and boring, but it might be painful as we limit spending to set money aside for investment opportunities that come are way.

Revisiting the parable of the talents

First, we have to understand that investing is a good thing. Dr. Anderson's book tells the historical economic story behind the parable of the talents. It really was about money and investing.

> The details are not given in the gospels, but from history we do know some of the investment options available to them. In the early Roman Empire, the government raised money by selling contract bonds or taxation bonds. In other words, you could invest money in the government and earn dividends on your stock. This was happening before Jesus was born and continued long afterwards. The servants in the parable took money and invested it in what could be

considered the world's system. The opportunities were available to anyone with the initiative and the awareness to notice them and take advantage of them.

It helps us to see that Jesus was referencing the financial markets of the day which in principle are not that much different than the markets we have today.

Create wealth

In chapter three we discussed the need to be fully convinced that God wants us to prosper financially. If we are convinced of this, we will have the godly desire that will drive us to change and take creative actions and not feel guilty when God prospers us.

One of the reasons people feel guilty about prospering financially is because they are told there is a fixed amount of money in the world and the more they have, the less someone else has. This is not good economics. It is not a fixed economic pie. If you have a bigger piece of the pie it does not mean someone else has a smaller piece. The truth is most nations of the world have a growing economic pie. That is why Gross Domestic Product (GDP) increases every year except in times of recession.

A number of modern economic theories view man's primary role on the earth as a consumer. A biblical worldview gives us a different picture. We were meant to be producers first and consumers second. In Genesis chapter one it states that God created us to be fruitful and productive. We should not look at consumption as our primary purpose in life. This is a secular worldview that lacks any sense of destiny … eat, drink and be merry for tomorrow we die.

The secular person views an additional child in a family as another mouth to feed rather than another person to contribute to the production of food. This view is based on an expectation of scarcity and limitation. The same person will say there is not enough water in the world for the growing population. The truth is we do not lack for water on the earth. The oceans are full of water. The challenge is to obtain drinkable water, which drives us to discover the needed technology for water purification. The lack is not water; the lack is ideas and technology.

A few years ago I had the opportunity to visit the Cape of Good Hope in South Africa. I watched the forty to fifty-foot waves repeatedly crash against the rocks one after another. The ocean spray went hundreds of feet in the air after impacting the rocks. It struck me that we do not have a power problem on the earth. We have a problem with harnessing power. It is a technology problem not a lack problem. The earth has plenty of untapped resources that are available to us.

This is important when discussing investing because if we feel like we are competing with others for a limited piece of the pie, it will stifle our creativity. If we think that having one nation prosperous makes the others poor, it will limit our desire to grow our nation. The truth is every nation has an equal chance to prosper. We should live in a world of abundance, not one of limitations. With a little bit of creativity we can find a way for a win/win versus a win/lose. Jesus had an abundance mentality. He said the "fields are white unto harvest." An abundance mentality means that rather than seeing life as a competition with only one winner, you see it as an unquenchable fountain of ever enlarging opportunity, resources and wealth.

If we have an abundance mentality, we will not compare ourselves to others and will be genuinely happy for their success. We are not trying to "keep up with the Joneses," we are on a mission from God to fund his kingdom. It is between us and him. It has nothing to do with comparison. We can learn from others, but we are not in competition with them.

I believe part of the reason that God had the children of Israel take a Sabbath year every seven years was to cause them to stop the systematic, year after year, planting and harvesting so they could think creatively. Because they were required to stop working for a year, they had time to reflect on what they were doing and how they were doing it. These years of rest also caused them to spend time building relationships that no doubt gave them ideas to incorporate after the Sabbath year was over and work began again.

How hard do you want to work?

To create wealth we cannot think in terms of an hourly paycheck. If we are putting our time in and waiting for our monthly paycheck, we will have our needs met but we will not prosper. Our paycheck will be limiting and not allow us to do all the things God has asked us to do.

For example, as long as we are driving a truck making deliveries we will only be able to make so much money in one week, because we are limited in the number of deliveries we can make by the hours of the week. If we are going to prosper making deliveries, we need to find a way to get more trucks on the road. Or consider the difference between a laborer who works for pay and a farmer who plants seeds. To be a successful farmer, you must develop a sense of dominion. You have to be confident that your mind can produce more than your hands.

Let us say you have the choice between selling pens for a living or shining shoes. The amount of money to be made shining shoes is capped by the hours of the day. The amount of money to be made from selling pens is not limited because someone else produces them and you can order any amount to be sold. Pens could be marketed on an Internet site that takes orders from around the world twenty-four hours a day without you even expending any energy.

We need to consider the value of our time when deciding our investment strategies. Real estate investing can be very lucrative but it will require time. In the same way, operating a small business is a very time intensive investment as well but is many times the surest vehicle to financial blessing.

Investing in markets via mutual funds, real estate investment trusts and other financial vehicles are both time efficient and profitable. They reduce the time needed to figure out investments. It has often been stated that instead of us working for dollars, our dollars are working for us. However, there are some parameters that we must be aware of while investing in markets.

Buying and selling in financial markets

If we believe that the natural state of creation is growth and reproduction, we will invest in financial markets. Growth is the natural order of things. One financial adviser puts it like this, "Trees grow." In other words optimism and planning for long term results are usually rewarded. Growth is the natural state of economics. Proverbs 25: 25–27 speaks to this truth that the natural state of things is to grow.

> When the hay is removed and new growth appears and the grass from the hills is gathered in, lambs will provide you with clothing, and the goats with the price of a field. You will have plenty of goats' milk to feed your family and to nourish your female servant.

In other words investing in markets allow you to increase wealth over a long period of time from an arm's length. There are pitfalls however: Greed and fear.

Greed and fear

Many observers are fond of saying that markets are driven by greed and fear. That means they are emotionally driven and this causes people to lose discipline in their investment goals. I understand that Warren Buffet says investing is like dieting, easy to understand but difficult to do. Unfortunately the emotional roller coaster drives investors to lose money because they sell when markets are down or going down and buy when markets are up or going up. Just the opposite of what they should do.

The most effective market investing does not track and respond to the daily gyrations of markets but focuses on the long term growth over time. This is one reason it is important for you to have a plan and stick to it. The most productive investments in markets are those that are focused on gains over the long term. Remember, "Trees grow." This is called passive investing. Buy some securities and expect over time that they will make money and increase in value.

Greed

Greed will push an investor to think they have some special insider information and can predict what markets do. Markets generally have the current economic information calculated in to the current pricing. The market does not have the unexpected information calculated in and that is what makes it volatile and susceptible to insider trading. Rapid, reactionary trading is called active investing and accumulates multiplied fees and taxes that passive investing does not.

What we have to remember about buying and selling in markets is every time we are selling because we think the time is right, someone else on the other end of the trade is thinking this is the right time to buy. So it really does put us in competition with them, trying to outsmart them or beat them, rather than holding on to shares for a long period of time and growing with the investment.

Fear

Fear causes people to panic when the market is dropping. Obviously this makes for poor long-term results. The experienced investors beat the inexperienced investors in down markets, because the inexperienced investors panic and sell and the experienced investors buy when the market is down. History has shown that the best time to buy is during times of distress, however very few have the courage, means and discipline to do this.

Be realistic about expected investment returns. Generally speaking 10 percent is the maximum benchmark over the long term. If anyone is offering you significantly more than this, it should raise a red flag of warning for you. Do not expect to beat the market averages. Your long-term investments should be based on buying and holding good investments, not trying to time when you should be in or out of a particular investment.

Diversify

One of the keys that many investment advisors will tell us was actually published in the Bible long before the advisors became aware of it. Diversify. Read Ecclesiastes 11:1, 6.

> Ship your grain across the sea; after many days you may receive a return. Invest in seven ventures, yes, in eight; you do not know what disaster may come upon the land.... Sow your seed in the morning, and at evening let your hands not be idle, for you do not know which will succeed, whether this or that, or whether both will do equally well.

The reason to diversify and spread your investments among different areas and venues of finance is that it minimizes risk. If we hold a variety of investments that perform differently in various environments, then we are protected from loss if one area goes bad. This minimizes risk. We should hold a variety of investments that perform differently in various environments.

Invest where you have confidence

During the credit crisis of the late 1990s, the Chinese came through almost completely unscathed. The credit crisis and ensuing world recession was caused by some complex financial instruments that the Chinese did not totally understand. Since they did not have confidence to invest in these financial instruments they were saved the hardship suffered by banks and institutions around the world. We could criticize them and say that they are not very sophisticated investors or we could learn from them. They did not overstep into an area where they did not have confidence, and it saved them huge losses.

I meet some people making money in business and they say the best way to make money is starting a business. They say real estate is a "no win" venture. I meet other people making money in real estate and they say business is a "no win" venture. Guess what? They have found where they have grace to be fruitful.

A friend of mine is a manager in a metal working plant that produces metal fixtures from different kinds of metals for manufacturing. He is investing in metal commodities. He understands the supply and demand of these metals and it is working well for him. He has a natural authority in this area. I would never have confidence to do that.

Another friend of mine has a drafting business. He worked in construction for many years before that. He is now investing money in rental properties. This is working out well for him because he knows the industry and has a natural authority there. Where do you have confidence to invest? Is there an area where your parents or family members have found success? What are the natural gifts God has given you? Are you good with numbers? Good with people? Move toward these areas.

This same principle applies if you are buying stocks. Buy stock in the companies you know and trust. I mean, look around your house. What is the brand of your clothes washer? Do you like it? Does it work well? Where do you like to stop for coffee? Buy stock in that company. Do not buy stock in a gold mine on another continent that you have never seen.

That sums up the hot tips for investing in markets. Now we will consider real estate as an investment tool.

Small Group Study Questions

1.   What is meant by the term "trees grow"?

2.   Why is it a better business to sell pens than give massages?

3.   What effect does greed have on investing?

4.   What effect does fear have on investing?

5.   What are some areas in which you have confidence to invest?

Chapter 17

Acres of Diamonds

In the years following the Civil War in the United States, a pastor by the name of Russell Cronwell traveled America and stirred millions of people with a story he told. The name of the story is Acres of Diamonds. It is the story of an Indian merchant who had been told by a prophet that he would become rich if he would only seek his treasure. So the merchant traveled the world in search of treasure only to return home after many years disappointed and defeated. As he came back to his abandoned house he needed a drink of water, but the well on the property was covered with silt. So he took out his shovel and dug a new well. As he was digging he struck what became the world's greatest diamond mine. His fortune was not "out there" somewhere, but right under his nose all along.

Generally speaking the best opportunity could be right under your nose. I love it when God asked Moses, "What is in your hand?" God did not ask this because he did not know. He asked it because he wanted to direct Moses attention to use what he had already been given.

God loves real estate

Land is important to God's plan for his children. One of the first things God did in establishing a covenant with Abraham was give him land. Previous to this, Abraham did not have a homeland. Abraham's father and his family were pastoral nomads, wandering from place to place for varying periods of time. His father worshiped idols in a city dedicated to wickedness. Abraham was told by God to go out into a place in which he would receive his inheritance. It was later referred to at the Promised "land." It was land! In Genesis 12:1 it refers to the "land" God had for Abraham.

The Lord had said to Abram, "Leave your country, your people and your father's household and go to the land I will show you."

God gave this nomad a land to call his own and to build in with his descendants. He gave Abraham and his family the land of Israel as a unique homeland where his descendants were supposed to create the nation that was the model for the world. Physical land was central to God's plan to prosper Abraham.

We see a parallel lesson if we study the great Native American tribes from North America. The tribes along the East Coast were less transient and would stay in one place and farm the land as well as hunt. They tended to survive and prosper. Those tribes along the West Coast were nomadic hunters who traveled to seasonal hunting grounds. They were more likely to starve and die. They could never prosper because they never settled down and stayed in one place. Simply stated, when you are a nomad there is only so much you can carry, so it is hard to prosper.

There is something about land that is really important to God. The story of Ruth is, of course, a great love story. But it is also the story of God giving a woman physical land. God took her from gleaning leftovers along the edge of the field to the owner of the field. When she married Boaz, who owned the field, she became an owner of the very field she formerly gleaned in as a pauper.

Land creates capital

In the United States, the number one way that people finance new business ventures is by borrowing money against their house, which is of course located on land. So the best preparation for starting a business is to purchase a house and start paying it off. This will eventually build equity that will allow you to finance a business start up. Small business start ups create 70 percent of new jobs. Most of these businesses are family businesses, and as with Abraham and his sons, land is often central to birthing these new businesses.

In light of this link between economic development and land ownership in first world nations, it is important to look at the developing and former Communist nations of the world that are hamstrung from economic growth because of weak or nonexistent property rights. For prosperity to come to these nations, one of the first needs is to improve the laws governing property ownership so people can own property free and clear.

Sadly, in many nations of the world, a piece of real estate might have as many as five or ten different people claiming ownership of it, and there is no functioning system to determine who owns the deed to this land. One person claims his uncle gave him the land, another says he bought it for an amount of money from the neighbor; another claims it is theirs because they have been squatting on it for the last few years. As long as it cannot be determined who the actual owner of the land is and that it is free of claims against it, no bank will accept this land as collateral for a loan that might be used to start a business. Established and legal property rights systems can create capital and economic lift for everyone.

Fernando De Soto in his book, T*he Mystery of Capital*, describes this predicament.

> Imagine a country where nobody can identify who owns what, addresses cannot be easily verified, people cannot be made to pay their debts, resources cannot conveniently be turned into money, ownership cannot be divided into shares, descriptions of assets are not standardized and cannot be easily compared, and the rules that govern property vary from neighborhood to neighborhood or even street to street. You have just put yourself into the life of a developing country or former communist nation. More precisely, you have imagined life for 80 percent of its population ... 80 percent of the world is undercapitalized; people cannot draw economic life from their buildings (or any other asset) to generate capital. In Haiti, according to our surveys, 68 percent of city dwellers and 97 percent of people in the countryside live in housing to which nobody has a clear legal title. Legal property empowers individuals in any culture.

In contrast to this are Western nations that have developed the structures that allow property to be leveraged for economic development. Again from *The Mystery of Capital:*

The recognition and integration of extra legal property rights was a key element in the United States becoming the most important market economy and producer of capital in the world.... The six effects of an integrated property process mean that Westerners' houses no longer merely keep the rain and cold out. Endowed with representational existence, these houses can now lead a parallel life, doing economic things that could not have been done before.

Citizens of advanced nations are thus able to split their assets into shares, each of which can be owned by different persons, with different rights to carry out different functions. Thanks to formal property, a single factory can be held by countless investors, who can divest themselves of their property without affecting the integrity of the physical asset.

Perhaps rather than sending billions of dollars of aid to developing nations, we should provide finances for their young people to get legal training in property law to put these legal structures in place so the people can prosper. Such laws also protect ownership as many people(s) have suffered the taking of their land unjustly as well. This is stealing, and God cannot bless land that is taken from others unjustly. Though some cultures celebrate common ownership of land, in most cases this does not allow for economic prosperity. The idea of private property rights is embedded in the Ten Commandments. "You shall not steal" underlines this principle. God's plan is individual ownership and stewardship.

Land is on God's heart. It is a key to how he prospers his people. Our experience has been one where the most significant increases in our personal net worth have come as the result of real estate transactions. If you do not own land it is very likely that God wants to help you get some. If you own land, possibly God wants to give you more. Rick Joyner states that the great thing about real estate is that it is "real." It not a piece of paper related to a stock option purchase in a market somewhere. It is real. You can go there and walk on it. You can grow corn on it if you want.

Principles for the Successful Investor

There are a few things you will need to learn to be a successful investor.

1. **You have to understand basic accounting**. As odd as this may seem, most schools do not teach the basic accounting tools needed to develop wealth. *Rich Dad, Poor Dad* by Richard Kiyosaki is the best book I would recommend to learn basic accounting.

2. **Focus on buying assets.** These are items or financial instruments that retain or increase in value. Do not buy items that lose their value over time. Money is a store of value. Money represents your time and efforts. Take money and put it into things that will retain or increase in value.

3. **It is important to learn how investments work while you are not working.** Remember the farmer who has his crops growing while he is sleeping. How can your money work for you separate from your blood sweat and tears?

4. **You must learn the tax laws** or hire someone who does. This is necessary so that the wealth you accumulate can actually be used for the purpose God intended it and not given needlessly to government taxes.

5. **Saving is a prerequisite for investing.** Living within your means and saving to invest will develop the discipline needed to be a successful investor.

6. **Do your homework before you buy an investment.** Get your financial advice from a fee only advisor who does not profit from selling you an investment instrument.

7. **Do not expect to beat the market averages.** Your long-term investments should be based on buying and holding good investments, not trying to time when you should be in or out of a particular investment.

8. **Consider the value of your time when deciding your investment strategies.** Real estate investing and running a small business are the most time intensive investments. Mutual funds are both time efficient and profitable.

9. **Look for investments that can accumulate value without your constant attention to them.** If you start a business shining shoes, then even if you are the fastest shoe shiner in the world, your income potential is still limited by the hours in the week.

10. **Think long term.** What are you confident to own for the next five to ten years?

The Fox Story

With all the due diligence, common sense and practical wisdom that I have been emphasizing in approaching wealth generation, we also need to rely on the direction of God's spirit. Jesus did come along and tell the disciples, who were experienced fishermen, to throw their nets on the other side of the boat. They followed his direction and pulled in a miraculous catch. Let me give an example.

I have a building with two rental units in it. I experienced a genuine crisis because neither one of the tenants was paying and neither one of the tenants wanted to get out of their apartment. Realizing that we were not helping the individuals by letting them stay there, we started the painfully slow legal process to evict them.

As I was praying one day about these units, God showed me a picture of a red fox curled up and sleeping under one of the apartments. I could not tell which apartment it was but I was able to discern that it was not a good fox; it represented an evil presence that was resident in one of the units. I immediately responded by commanding the fox to get out of my apartments and to get out of my town in Jesus' name. I did not want this same spirit to just move into another location in our town. So I just made the verbal declaration I felt the Lord was directing me to make and moved on to other things I had to do that day.

The next day I had to drop something off at the building. To my surprise the renters on the one side approached me and said they were moving out. They came and proudly told me that they were moving to another city in our area. I did not have to wonder which side "the fox" was sleeping under, clearly this spirit of darkness was leaving town as I commanded it to do the day before. So in business, we must stay tuned in to the voice of the

Holy Spirit. He wants to help us. John 14:16 calls the Holy Spirit our helper and he will help us with our business as well.

Wind and hail

Here is another example. A friend of mine and his partner are in the construction business. They do remodeling of homes in need of repair or upgrade. Business was a little slow a couple of years ago, so my friend felt like the Lord was prompting him to put a sign advertising their business on a street corner in a neighborhood near where he lived. It seemed like a totally random act of advertising to the point of him questioning why he should do it. But he followed through because he felt a prompting of the Lord.

Within a few weeks of him putting out the sign, a violent storm came through the area with large amounts of hail accompanying it. The hail damage was extensive. In many cases, it shredded the soft vinyl that was used by many builders for house siding in our area. The damage from the storm required repair, and many of the people in need of repair called my friend's business because of the storm. They were swamped with hail damage repair business.

Did God cause the storm? I do not think so, but he motivated my friend to put out a sign before the storm's damage. This sounds like God's supernatural direction to me.

Norm Schlemmer is a church leader and a businessman. He has gained significant net worth by allowing the Holy Spirit to be his teacher. He told me, "The real key as a believer is to have a working relationship with the Holy Spirit. His role is to lead and guide. Everything that I own and have accumulated is a direct result of the Holy Spirit speaking to me and directing me. My goal early on was to be in ministry only. I have discovered that my five businesses have gained me more access into the community than the ministry ever did. The people have been impressed by what I have built, not what I have preached. When they ask how I did it, I tell them about Jesus. It has opened many doors for witnessing. Every business, house, airplane and property that I have owned or own is a direct result of the Spirit of God speaking and directing the strategy. My goal is not to amass money to buy bigger homes, drive more expensive cars and airplanes, but to help people and further the kingdom. I think this is the way it is supposed to be."

NOTES

1   Russel Cronwell, *Acres of Diamonds*
2   Hernando de Soto, *The Mystery of Capital: Why Capitalism Triumphs in the West and Fails Everywhere Else* (New York: Basic Books, 2000).

Small Group Study Questions

1. Discuss the concept of "God loves real estate."

2. What did owning land mean to Ruth?

3. What do property rights have to do with creating wealth?

4. Discuss the list of investing tips. Which ones were new to you? How will you apply them?

5. How does God supernaturally lead us with investing?

Chapter 18

Your City Can Prosper Too

In the late 1940s and early 1950s, a young man named Roger Bannister from Oxford University began to have a dream—to run the 1600 meter race in under four minutes. It had been attempted by many runners but it was a barrier that no one had been able to break. Roger became convinced that it was possible. No matter what others told him, he simply would not believe their words, for he believed the barrier could be broken.

On May 5, 1954, Bannister broke the barrier running the 1600 meter race in under four minutes. Amazingly enough, before the year was over a number of other athletes ran the same race in under four minutes. In one race, five men broke the record at one time. What had happened? The barrier to accomplishing this great athletic feat did not exist in their physical bodies, it was in their minds. It was in their thinking. One person broke through into a new possibility and others quickly followed.

What barriers do we have in our minds that keep us from accomplishing all that God has for us? From the scriptures we have already learned that we will prosper as our thinking prospers. But let's take that a step further. What if our prosperous thinking can be combined with others to impact our city or the region in which we live?

Psalm 128 is a song that was literally sung by the children of Israel as they traveled up the hills to the old city of Jerusalem for their annual feasts and celebrations. It was a song of joy celebrating God's blessing on vocation, home and family. One of the things they sang about was the prosperity of the city they loved...Jerusalem. Let's read it.

> "How joyful are those who fear the Lord—all who follow his ways! You will enjoy the fruit of your labor. How joyful and prosperous you will be. Your wife will be like a fruitful grapevine, flourishing within your home. Your children will be like vigorous young olive trees as they sit around your table. That is the Lord's blessing for those who fear him. May the Lord continually bless you from Zion. May you see Jerusalem prosper as long as you live. May you live to enjoy your grandchildren. May Israel have peace!"

Though Jerusalem holds a special place in the hearts of many Christians, most of us do not live in Jerusalem. God wants to prosper us in the city where we physically live. We need jobs. Our neighbors need jobs. Our children will need jobs.

When Jeremiah was speaking of God's desires for the children of Israel in exile, he commissioned them to seek the prosperity of the city in which they were living.

> Also, seek the peace and prosperity of the city to which I have carried you into exile. Pray to the Lord

for it, because if it prospers, you too will prosper (Jeremiah 29:7).

Many Christians are fond of stating that heaven is their home and they are just visitors here on earth. Though this is true in the light of eternity, God's desire is for us to see prosperity come to the cities, villages and towns in which we live.

Can a whole city prosper?

Is this possible? Can a whole city prosper? Can a whole city be lifted out of poverty? There are those who are trying. Listen to Steve Fricke's story from Wilmington, Ohio. Steve is both a pastor and a businessman. A couple of years previous to this, a major employer in their community closed, which eliminated ten thousand jobs from the area. Steve writes:

> With our community experiencing double-digit unemployment the local businesses have suffered. For more than two years the local community pastors have been meeting weekly to pray for spiritual and economic revival. We specifically are asking for the abandoned store fronts and factories to be refilled with prosperous kingdom-minded business leaders. And we are asking for God's creativity to be released among area believers to start new businesses and fill the old ones.
>
> As a business person myself, I recognize the need to encourage the business owners to dig the ditches in preparation for God's provision to be released. We can sit around complaining and worry about what is

going to happen to us or we can dig some ditches. For some, this means hitting the pavement again to make sales calls or expand market territory. For others it means dreaming again about what their business can become and the importance it carries in the community and in the kingdom. By that I mean keeping people employed and continuing to contribute to the overall economy. Some may need to go back to what they did in the beginning to make their business a success. But the need is encouragement for their business talents to be released in expectation of God's provision.

Specifically, we have commissioned two retired businessmen to visit each establishment owned by a Christian. One of these men is a retired banker and the other a retired customer service representative. They are praying with the business owners and their employees. They are asking God for prophetic words for that specific business. They are offering their experience and expertise in giving ideas and consumer perspectives so the owners can make adjustments if necessary. And they are helping the owners connect with others who have ideas or have overcome obstacles and who might offer additional encouragement. I personally have been able to assist one establishment in a cost-savings plan that yielded the owner more than nine thousand dollars in savings this year.

Second, the community pastors have yearly held a "Be the Church Day" where our congregations come together as one force with no church labels to do service projects around our city. This year we are concentrating on blessing our downtown business district. We will clean, paint, wash windows, do repairs, sweep sidewalks, refresh planters and mulch, clean restrooms and do anything else that will let the owners know in a practical way that we care and we are praying for them.

When you are in the desert and all you see around you is dry sand, you need a word of encouragement to dig the ditches for God's provision. He is good and faithful always, and I am confident the ditches will run with fresh provisional water in Wilmington again.

Steve's reference to digging ditches is taken from 2 Kings 3:16 where Elisha told the Kings who were in need of water to dig ditches. They followed his direction and the next day the ditches were filled with the water they needed. The following is another example of a village prospering. This example is set in a developing nation.

Hesbone Odindo leads the DOVE churches in the Kisumu region of Western Kenya. They first started a small group in 2005 in Hesbone's home village of Kadawa, approximately four hundred km from Nairobi. This group grew into a church called Restoration Community Church, which was officially launched in January 2006 with thirty members. Today, the church has multiplied into three churches with close to one thousand people attending. But Hesbone and his wife Violet do not stop with just spiritual transformation of church members.They have a vision for physical transformation as well.

They worked and obtained financing to oversee the transition of village swampland into banana tree groves. Because of the growth of the church and the addition of the banana trees, more than ten new jobs were created. New bore holes were drilled for clean water for the villagers to drink, which eliminated Cholera that had previously claimed five to ten lives each year. Because of the high number of people whose immune systems were weakened by HIV, historically four people a week died from malaria. The Kadawa church introduced mosquito nets which cut the malaria death rate to one per month. As Hesbone followed the call of God to his native village, his village began to prosper.

God's presence brings a sense of blessing to individuals and to the place where they live. If we examine the ark of the covenant in the Old Testament we find something interesting.

> The ark of God remained with the family of Obed-Edom in his house for three months, and the Lord blessed his household and everything he had (1 Chronicles 13:14).

The ark, which represented God's presence, brought prosperity wherever it went. So if God's people prosper, then the cities in which they live can prosper too.

Joseph's prosperity affected the places he lived

Earlier in the book, we looked at the life of Joseph and saw that he had a prosperous soul. He often encountered opposition, but he always found a way to prosper. In addition, whatever physical location Joseph was in seemed to prosper as well; first Potiphar's household, then the prison where Joseph stayed and finally the whole nation of Egypt. According to the Bible, Joseph's brothers sold him as a slave to a traveling caravan when he was a teenager. From there, he was traded off as a slave to an Egyptian official named Potiphar. This presented a huge challenge, but not for long, as we read in Genesis.

> The Lord was with Joseph and he prospered, and he lived in the house of his Egyptian master. When his master saw that the Lord was with him and that the Lord gave him success in everything he did, Joseph found favor in his eyes and became his attendant. Potiphar put him in charge of his household, and he entrusted to his care everything he owned. From the time he put him in charge of his household and of all that he owned, the Lord blessed the household of the Egyptian because of Joseph. The blessing of the Lord was on everything Potiphar had, both in the house and in the field. So he left in Joseph's care everything he had; with Joseph in charge, he did not concern himself with anything except the food he ate (Genesis 39:2-6).

Potiphar saw the blessing in Joseph's life, and it convinced him to put his whole household in Joseph's hands. He saw that everything he put under Joseph's authority multiplied and prospered. Potiphar entrusted everything he had to Joseph's care. Eventually, Potiphar did not even know how much money he had accumulated. God's blessing on Joseph was making Potiphar rich. But just when it seemed like Joseph had advanced as far as he could, God allowed something to happen that sent Joseph to prison; only to see the prison blessed and become a better place.

But while Joseph was there in the prison, the Lord was with him; he showed him kindness and granted him favor in the eyes of the prison warden. So the warden put Joseph in charge of all those held in the prison, and he was made responsible for all that was done there. The warden paid no attention to anything under Joseph's care, because the Lord was with Joseph and gave him success in whatever he did (Genesis 39:20–23).

Was the prison a better place to work as a guard or even be a prisoner when Joseph was in charge? Somehow I think it was. The rest of the story is that Joseph's prosperous soul and advancing mindset soon opened up the door for him to lead Egypt during a very challenging time of natural disaster. The whole nation was blessed by Joseph's leadership. Joseph personally prospered and so those in Potiphar's household, the prison and eventually all of Egypt prospered. We must change our thinking first and eventually our city and region will prosper as well.

Christianity helped the middle class emerge

Historically, Christianity has brought much prosperity to society. Alvin Schmidt points out that before Christianity the Greek/Roman viewpoint of physical labor was very low. It was only suitable for slaves and the lower classes. The Christian view of labor and work as honorable and God-pleasing was in direct conflict with the Greek/Roman idea. This view set them apart in honoring work, but also they prospered economically because of their strong work ethic. Before Christians brought dignity to work and labor, there was not much of a middle class. People were either rich or poor, and the poor were slaves. But with the spread of Christianity, the economic phenomenon of the middle class arose, which is now present in all Western societies.[1]

Francis Schaeffer points out one of the practical results of Christianity transforming the workplace during the time of the Reformation. The result was that all the vocations in life came to have dignity. The vocation of honest merchant or housewife had as much value as the position of king, which was a radical thought for leaders in that time and a welcome relief to the followers of that day.[2]

Government officials are sometimes called the city fathers. Fathers want their sons to succeed. It seems appropriate that those in political offices work for the good and prosperity of the city. The following is the prayer that William Penn offered for the city of Philadelphia. It is still inscribed on the outside wall of City Hall in Philadelphia.

> And thou Philadelphia the virgin settlement of this province named before thou wert born, what care, what service, what travail have there been to bring thee forth and preserve thee from such as would abuse and defile thee. O that thou mayest be kept from the evil that would overwhelm thee, that faithful to the God of thy mercies in the life of righteousness, thou mayest be preserved to the end. My soul prays to God for thee that thou mayest stand in the day of trial, that thy children may be blest of the Lord and thy people saved by His power.

This was a prayer for the prosperity of the city. In 2008 as a sitting, elected school board member in our local school district, I had the opportunity to pray a prayer of blessing and prosperity over a new middle school building we were opening. This same prayer was then mounted on the wall inside the main lobby of the building.

An intercessor friend of mine recently met with the mayor of a large United States city of six million people. The input he gave him was to say a blessing over the city each morning:

> Through the blessing of the upright a city is exalted, but by the mouth of the wicked it is destroyed (Proverbs 11:11).

Many times local citizens say negative things about their city, but a prosperous person will speak blessing over his city. However, it does take time for a whole city to prosper. I know a businessman who is fond of saying, "If you are lost thirty miles in the woods, you have to walk thirty miles to get out."

If we, or the population of a whole city, have been thinking one way for many years, it will take some time to reverse this. It is possible, but it is not easy and does not happen by accident. Not only will it take time, but it will take like-minded individuals collectively believing for the city or region to prosper.

NOTES

1   Alvin J. Schmidt, *How Christianity Changed the World* (Michigan: Zondervan, 2004),

2   Francis A. Schaeffer, *How Should We Then Live?* (Illinois: Crossway Books, 2005).

Small Group Study Questions

1. How does God's presence bring blessing to individuals and to the place where they live?

2. How has Christianity historically brought prosperity to society?

3. Make a list of people you know who could be involved in seeing your city prosper.

4. How did Joseph's prosperity affect the people around him?

5. What are some words to promote prosperity that people can speak over their city? Practice these words by speaking them over your city.

Chapter 19

Don't Deny Reality— Change It!

Remember the story at the beginning of this book about the veteran missionary who told his wife and children that they would always be poor because of their call to missions? His words bore the fruit of poverty and lack in his family even years after they were back from the mission field. He felt the Lord prompting him to retract those words. This spiritual principle is simply stated in Proverbs 18.

> From the fruit of his mouth a man's stomach is filled; with the harvest from his lips he is satisfied. The tongue has the power of life and death, and those who love it will eat its fruit (Proverbs 18:20–21).

Does it really matter what we say about my finances?

This is a very good and logical question. I will attempt to answer this question in a concise, biblical manner by examining some scriptures that teach how the words we speak affect all areas of our lives, including our finances.

God puts a lot of importance on what we say. There are many scriptures that mention this. The scripture that we commonly use to lead people to faith in Jesus Christ, Romans 10:9, indicates that we should not only believe in our hearts but also confess with our mouths to come into salvation. Even though we believe in our hearts, which is something that happens in the "unseen" world, it seems it is spiritually significant to speak the words out loud into the "seen" world in which we live. The words we speak are at the very core of the gospel of Jesus Christ.

In the beginning of the Bible, we find Genesis teaching that God created the world in six days by his words. He said, "Let there be light," and there literally was light created. As we study these scriptures, it appears that God's very words were the creative force that brought the world into existence.

Later, God changed Abram's name to Abraham. God started calling Abraham "the father of many" when he was not even the father of one son. He was not the father of anyone! Worse yet, by changing his name, God made Abraham call himself "the father of many" every time he introduced himself to someone or someone asked his name. Can you picture Abraham feeling a little embarrassed as he, a man without a son or daughter, spoke the words, "My name is 'Father of Many'?" Yet Abraham's faith-filled words eventually bore the fruit of making him the father of many. If God worked in Abraham's life by directing him to speak words declaring his destiny, we have to ask the question, "Does God want us to do this today?" As you read through this chapter, I believe your answer will be a resounding "yes."

Many other Bible figures used this biblical truth of spoken declaration when expecting their current situation and circumstances to change. It worked for them. David had the following words to say at his encounter with Goliath:

David said to the Philistine, "You come against me with sword and spear and javelin, but I come against you in the name of the Lord Almighty, the God of the armies of Israel, whom you have defied. This day the Lord will hand you over to me, and I'll strike you down and cut off your head. Today I will give the carcasses of the Philistine army to the birds of the air and the beasts of the earth, and the whole world will know that there is a God in Israel. All those gathered here will know that it is not by sword or spear that the Lord saves; for the battle is the Lord's, and he will give all of you into our hands" (1 Samuel 17:45–47).

This was not a silent prayer to God. In fact, he did not direct these words to God at all. David said these words to Goliath, his enemy. "I will strike you down and cut off your head." That's bold. He was declaring faith-filled words about what God wanted to do. The events he spoke of had not actually happened as yet. However they did come to pass.

You are the prophet of your own life

What about Jesus cursing the fig tree in the gospel of Mark? He spoke to the fig tree. He did not pull it up. He did not ask his disciples to cut it down. No, his words were enough to cause it to die by the time he returned that way.

Jesus continued on after finding the dead fig tree to teach about faith. He underlined again the importance of faith-filled words and how battles are won and victories gained by using them.

"Have faith in God," Jesus answered. "I tell you the truth, if anyone says to this mountain, 'Go, throw yourself into the sea,' and does not doubt in his heart but believes that what he says will happen, it will be done for him. Therefore I tell you, whatever you ask for in prayer, believe that you have received it, and it will be yours" (Mark 11:22–24).

We are to say to the mountain, "Throw yourself into the sea." Mountains are the things that stand in the way of us fulfilling God's will for our lives. Jesus told us to speak (out loud) to the mountains in our lives.

You may remember that Jesus called Simon by the name "Peter." He called Peter a rock when it looked like he was anything but a solid guy that could be involved in building the kingdom of God. I believe when Jesus said those words, it actually released the power that helped make Peter into "the rock" that he would become.

How about this scripture in Romans, chapter 4, that describes God and how he does things on the earth.

Therefore, the promise comes by faith, so that it may be by grace and may be guaranteed to all Abraham's offspring—not only to those who are of the law but also to those who are of the faith of Abraham. He is the father of us all. As it is written: "I have made you a father of many nations." He is our father in the sight of God, in whom he believed—the God who gives life to the dead and calls things that are not as though they were (Romans 4:16-17).

This scripture teaches that God himself calls things "that are not as though they were." It sounds a lot like what God did in Genesis when he created the heavens, the earth, light, man and so forth. Does this mean that he wants us to also speak creative, faith-filled words? Yes, I believe it does. When he is challenging us to speak out words of faith he is challenging us to co-create with him in our lives and in our areas of responsibility. I heard one person say it like this: "If you are not saying it, you are not creating it." This is how God operates. We see it again in Amos.

> Surely the Sovereign Lord does nothing without revealing his plan to his servants the prophets (Amos 3:7).

Why does he reveal plans to the prophets? So they can prophesy it. Say it. Speak it into existence. God has the prophets say it because they are his representatives on earth today and God is not physically here to say it himself. Let's take a close look at the following proverb:

> From the fruit of his lips a man is filled with good things as surely as the work of his hands rewards him (Proverbs 12:14).

To understand the truth presented in the verse, we must recognize that the Bible compares the hours we work and the paycheck we receive for the work with the results that come from our spoken words. As surely as you plant corn in the ground and it grows and produces a crop it is equally as sure that your faith-filled words will reward you with good things. The prophet Joel instructed the weak to "say" they are strong. Say it. You are the prophet of your own life.

I am not denying reality I am changing it

I have to admit though, in spite of all these scriptures, it still feels awkward to say "My debts are paid off," when I have a payment schedule in my desk drawer for loan payments. And yet, somehow when I say those words, faith rises up in my heart that the mountain of debt can and will be removed from my life. It is a spiritual principle, and it is not always easy to understand how it works. But it does work. I have to say it like this, I am not denying reality, I am changing it.

The passage 2 Corinthians 1:20–21 gives us some additional insight into how God's promises come to pass in our lives.

> For no matter how many promises God has made, they are "yes" in Christ. And so through him the "Amen" is spoken by us to the glory of God. Now it is God who makes both us and you stand firm in Christ.

The promises of God the Father are for us and Christ has given a "yes" to these promises. However, the "amen" is spoken by us. We must say the amen. Our declaration is essential to trigger His promises in our lives. As we align ourselves with the Father and Son, it completes the loop and becomes reality.

As an example, I remember distinctly the Holy Spirit prompting me to change the words I spoke about purchasing cars. Years ago while I was listening to a financial expert, I heard a recommendation to never purchase a new car because of the loss of value that happens when you take the car off the sales lot. For example you might purchase a new car for $20,000 but as soon as you drive it off the sales lot it is now a "used" car and only worth $17,000. I adopted this view as my own and proudly stated many times that I would never purchase a new car because it was such a bad deal. Consequently, we always owned and drove used cars, some of which had significant maintenance costs due to the amount of miles that were on the car.

I was driving in one of my used vehicles with a history of maintenance issues and I remembered the declaration I had spoken about never purchasing a new car. I sensed the Holy Spirit saying this to me, "What if I tell you to buy a new car?" I sat there in shock. I was not convinced it was, in fact, the Lord speaking but I responded by saying, "Yes, I would," because I am in submission to his will for my life. Still, I was so convinced buying a new car was a bad deal that I did not think he would ever tell me to do it.

As it turned out, this was what God was saying to me. In fact, I felt like I should start to say different words to replace my previous ones. So I started to say, "I will buy a new car," although only in private settings. I found that it was actually a little hard for me to get those words out of my mouth which underlined to me that I was probably on the right track. He was prompting me to replace my previous words, "I will never buy a new car," with different words which would produce a different outcome in my life. As you might expect within two years I purchased the first new car of my life. It was a little difficult for me to break through this ceiling that I put on my life by my own words, but I did it. I drove that new car without maintenance problems for many years. In using this example, I am not implying it is God's will for everyone to buy a new car. Since that time, I have purchased both new and used cars to meet the needs of our family.

In summary, it does matter what we say about our finances because the Bible says we will eat the fruit of our words. God speaks and things come to pass, and he wants us to speak forth his will for our lives and life situations and it will come to pass.

One more great example from the Bible is when the twelve spies returned from their trip to spy out the promised land. Ten of them said they could not conquer the land, but two—Joshua and Caleb—said God would give it to them. Joshua and Caleb got to see the land. They said God would give it to them, and they got to see it happen. The spies who said they were not strong enough to do it, did not do it.

So there are two sides to this coin. First, there are the words we have said that we should not have said such as the veteran missionary who spoke lack over his family. We need to delete those words and their power over our lives. Sometimes, as well, it is the words that others have spoken over our lives that need to be deleted. I will show you how to do this in a moment. The other side of the coin is represented by the faith-filled, creative words that the Holy Spirit is prompting us to say to change our present reality. Look at the exercise on the following page to engage both sides of the coin. Make a copy of the next page and answer the questions.

Take action

The following are words that we have spoken over ourselves or that others have spoken over us. We want to revoke the words, thus canceling their effect and breaking their power. Write down the negative words and draw a line through them, breaking their power in Jesus' name! Sign and date.

Example: "~~I will always work this dead-end job!~~"

a.

b.

c.

d.

These words have no power over me in Jesus' name!

Date:

Name:

What words will I use to replace the negative words?

Examples: "I will get ahead." "I will get a promotion" or "I will do what it takes to get a better paying job."

a.

b.

c.

d.

Boldly say the words you have written out loud right now! Repeat them three times.

Chapter 20

Live Long
and Prosper

Ephraim Tumusiime is a leader of leaders in the nation of Uganda. He leads a local church in Kampala but also gives oversight to many pastors throughout Uganda. Ephraim is a humble man who is doing great things for God in his nation. They are planting churches, building schools, feeding orphan children and bringing healing and restoration to a country that was brutalized by the dictator Idi Amin.

Ephraim and his wife, Jova, oversee more than fifty churches in Uganda. That is twice as many churches as two years ago. How could they double the number of churches in two years? Was it a sovereign move of God? Yes, God is moving there. Was it his great charismatic leadership? Yes, Ephraim is a good leader. Are they in the middle of a revival? Yes, the spiritual climate is good. However, part of the reason the number of churches has doubled is that someone spent twenty thousand dollars to buy Ephraim and Jova a new four-wheel drive vehicle so they could reach the remote rural areas of Uganda. The new vehicle is a real part of helping the kingdom of God expand in Uganda.

It is that simple—it takes money to extend the kingdom of God. Traveling ministers need transportation, cars need gas, buildings need electricity, people need to eat, the unreached need church planters, teen centers need gymnasiums, ministries need computers and the poor need jobs created for them. It takes money.

It is interesting to me that Genesis states there was gold in the Garden of Eden. Later, God moved on the Egyptians to give silver and gold to the children of Israel as they had requested before they left Egypt. God included gold rings in the blessing he gave to Job. In Haggai, gold and silver are mentioned in the same context as the glory of God.

> "I will shake all nations, and the desired of all na-
> tions will come, and I will fill this house with glory,"
> says the Lord Almighty. "The silver is mine and the
> gold is mine," declares the Lord Almighty. "The glory
> of this present house will be greater than the glory
> of the former house," says the Lord Almighty. "And
> in this place I will grant peace," declares the Lord
> Almighty (Haggai 2:7-9).

Have you read through the Song of Solomon? As you read the description of the bride you will find that she looks beautiful! Oh ... and interestingly enough, she is wearing gold and silver.

> Your cheeks are beautiful with earrings, your neck
> with strings of jewels. We will make you earrings of
> gold, studded with silver (Song of Solomon 1:10-12).

Relax. I am not suggesting we start the First Church of the Gold and Silver or a new theology of wealth. I just want to point out that God does not seem to mind having gold and silver around. In fact, he uses those for a paving material in the New Jerusalem. Clearly God's economy is different than ours.

We read in the Bible about an alabaster bottle of expensive perfume poured over Jesus' feet. Who was it that called it a waste? Judas. It was an act of worship, but he criticized it as wasteful excess. He even gave a spiritual reason not to do it ... so the money could be given to the poor. It was Judas who was missing the point. True waste is not noticing and enjoying what God put on earth for us. It is an act of worship to enjoy it.

Enjoy beauty and blessings

We will be more prosperous if we enjoy beauty and blessings. Do not apologize for God's blessing. Include beauty in your life; it will make you more prosperous. God made these things for us to enjoy. Ephraim should not have to apologize for the nice, new vehicle he received. He should enjoy the fact that he no longer gets stuck in the deep, muddy ditches in the Ugandan roadways.

So what about beauty? Our lives should both embrace and radiate the beauty of the Lord. God was the first artist, and we are his masterpiece. Beauty feeds your spirit. Why do I give my wife flowers? They just die anyway. No, it brings beauty into her day. It feeds her spirit. It changes our home.

It was my day off, and as usual I had more on my "to do" list than I could accomplish in two days. Stop here. Stop there. Drop this off. Talk to that person. Go to the bank. Rush in. Rush out. As I worked my way down the list, one of my stops was at a local greenhouse to buy spring flowers to plant around our house. I stopped and rushed into the greenhouse.

At first, I slowed down because there were so many different kinds of flowers from which to choose. Wow—so many different colors and sizes. Then someone behind me said, "Hi, Brian." It was a friend I hadn't seen for years. She asked me about my children. After giving her an update, I asked her about hers. As we went on our ways and I focused back on the flowers, I realized I was enjoying the beauty of the flowers and the quiet of the greenhouse. Then I thought about taking the flowers home and planting them with my six-year-old daughter when she got home from school. All of a sudden I did not want to rush the planting of the flowers. It seemed like I should just relax, slow down, enjoy the beauty of the flowers, and enjoy planting them with my daughter. I did.

Beauty feeds your soul

Jesus was talking about how to "not worry" when he said, "Consider the lilies of the valley. They do not labor or spin" (Luke 12:27). There is something about flowers and beauty in general that seems to cause worry and anxiety to leave. I like to say it this way: Beauty feeds your soul.

A family was building a home. It cost ten thousand dollars more to construct a cathedral ceiling instead of a traditional ceiling in their house. This added twenty thousand dollars to the resale value of the house. It added beauty to the house. Now when people enter the house their eyes are drawn to look up as with any cathedral. Is that such a bad thing? Maybe one day as the homeowner is sitting and looking up he gets an idea for a business. Now since they have more value in their home they can leverage that value for a loan to start the business that creates jobs for people who will get paid and go home and feed their kids with the money.

Is God's blessing just so you can buy a boat and go to the lake every weekend to relax? There is nothing wrong with a boat at the lake; in fact, God just might refresh you and give you some ideas to extend the kingdom while you are there. But remember, Jesus spoke about a man who built bigger barns for his harvest and propped up his feet to watch the world go by. We can never forget the purpose of the "more than enough." The truth is we do receive many blessings from the Lord for us and our families, and we should. But he will never let things keep you from fulfilling your purpose. It is not about what we receive, though we receive many things from our loving father, it is about what we give. Our end game is to extend the kingdom of God.

I have heard Christians try to have a theological discussion about what kind of car Jesus would have driven. Some try to prove he would have driven an expensive car, and others try to prove he would have driven a cheap car. Implied in this question is a justification for whatever car the individual wants to drive. I believe this is a fruitless discussion. If you are asking this question, you are thinking wrongly. Stop thinking about what you can get away with and start asking God what he is telling you to do. What is most effective in extending the kingdom?

As I mentioned earlier, I was an elected official on our local public school board. The people who serve on these kinds of boards have generally experienced a lot of success in their lives. When we go to dinner after a meeting, we do not go to a cheap restaurant. Is it a waste for me to spend that kind of money on a meal? I don't think so. I need to have those relationships to be an effective leader in our community. Also in those settings, I have often gained insights that have helped me be fruitful in other areas of my life and the kingdom.

I recently spent an evening with a businessman in the north of Poland. He was in an immediate need of five hundred thousand euros to maintain cash flow for his business. The Lord had given me some insight that would help his business. He thought nothing of taking a group of us to a very nice restaurant to talk. He was thinking about half a million Euros, so spending a few Euros on a nice meal for our party was not significant to him. It was money well spent if it helped his kingdom business succeed.

Time and money

Most people would say they would like more of both time and money. In this is a desire to be more fruitful and productive. This is a good and godly thing. We were created this way. The truth is there are many parallels between time and money. For example, we know it is better to invest money than to spend it. This would also be true of our time. It is better to invest time in people and projects that provide ongoing return than to spend it on things that are once and done.

The wealthy think the poor waste money, and the poor think the wealthy waste money. Who is right? A businessman sees it as very wasteful to take the time to change the oil in his cars. I have to agree. He could be out starting businesses and creating new jobs for people. A prosperous person realizes trying to save money on little things is usually a waste. I have noticed that poverty-minded people often will try to do everything themselves and save money. They never have enough time to finish, so there are often broken-down cars in their yard or unfinished parts of their house.

What is your time worth? Many of us do not put a monetary value on our own time. However we need to see that others do put a monetary value on our time. As an example, let's say you are in the United States and plan to travel from Philadelphia to Los Angeles. If you buy a bus ticket it will cost you $150, but it will take you thirty-six hours of time to get there. If you buy a plane ticket, it will cost you five hundred dollars, but the trip will take five hours to get there. If other people assign monetary value to our time, maybe it would benefit us to do the same.

Live long and prosper

Though it sounds idealistic, I do believe the Lord wants us to live long and prosper. He has created us to bear fruit and he put us on this earth for that reason. Prosperity means meeting the right people at the right time, climbing the right mountain in the right season, fighting the right battle with the right weapons, having the right people around us with the right skills, being at the right place to see opportunity and having the provisions there when we need them to fulfill our destiny. And then, help other people fulfill their destiny. This is how to be a prosperous Christian.

In my first book on biblical finance, *Prosperity with a Purpose,*[1] I focused on giving a picture of God as El Shaddai, the God of more than enough. Now in this book you have been given the practical tools to go beyond just knowing about El Shaddai. Develop a prosperous soul by using these tools as the Holy Spirit teaches you. I pray that you will be a good student as he teaches you to prosper.

NOTES

1 Sauder, *Prosperity with a Purpose*

Small Group Study Questions

1. According to the Bible, name some places where gold and silver can be found.

2. Give some examples of enjoying beauty and blessings?

3. Why is it important to enjoy beauty and blessings?

4. How are time and money related?

5. What are five keys for you to be a prosperous Christian?

APPENDIX A

El Shaddai Revealed In the Whole Bible

If abundant blessing is really the heart and nature of God, we should find it repeated throughout the Bible. That is precisely what we will see in this appendix.

Let's go to Exodus 36:3–7. Please notice the term "more than enough" as it appears in the following scriptures.

> They received from Moses all the offerings the Israelites had brought to carry out the work of constructing the sanctuary. And the people continued to bring freewill offerings morning after morning. So all the skilled craftsmen who were doing all the work on the sanctuary left their work and said to Moses, "The people are bringing *more than enough* for doing the work the Lord commanded to be done." Then Moses gave an order and they sent this word throughout the camp: "No man or woman is to make anything else as an offering for the sanctuary." And so the people were restrained from bringing more, because what they already had was *more than enough* to do all the work.

When is the last time you heard your pastor or any church leader say, "Stop giving. You're giving way too much?" When Moses started a building project, the Israelites were asked to participate by giving offerings. The people gave so much that Moses had to actually issue a decree instructing them to stop. I think most of us would agree the church today has not yet reached this stage.

How about Leviticus?

We have found Bible references to El Shaddai in Genesis and Exodus. Now let's look in Leviticus.

> I will look on you with favor and make you fruitful and increase your numbers, and I will keep my covenant with you. You will still be eating last year's harvest when you will have to move it out to make room for the new (Leviticus 26:9–10).

Verse 10 is what we are looking for: "You will still be eating last year's harvest when you will have to move it out to make room for this year's harvest." This sounds like more than enough to me. Last year's harvest was more than enough to meet the needs of the year. The surplus will have to be moved to make room for the new harvest.

Let your thinking be challenged

If your thinking is ruled by thoughts of poverty and lack, some of what I am saying might be hard to swallow. If this does not make sense right away, put it on the back burner, meditate on it and let it cook for a while. See what God shows you. It is a good thing for our thinking to be challenged as we look at the Word of God. We have to allow the Word of God to change us.

Listen to what God speaks to Moses and the children of Israel in Deuteronomy. Read these words:

> He will love you and bless you and increase your numbers. He will bless the fruit of your womb, the crops of your land—your grain, new wine and oil—the calves of your herds and the lambs of your flocks in the land that he swore to your forefathers to give you. You will be blessed more than any other people; none of your men or women will be childless, nor any of your livestock without young (Deuteronomy 7:13–14).

Does this sound like El Shaddai? "You will be blessed more than any other people." The key word here is "more." The next chapter states this even more clearly. Let's continue to read in Deuteronomy 8:6–11.

> Observe the commands of the Lord your God, walking in his ways and revering him. For the Lord your God is bringing you into a good land—a land with streams and pools of water, with springs flowing in the valleys and hills; a land with wheat and barley, vines and fig trees, pomegranates, olive oil and honey; a land where bread will not be scarce and you will lack nothing; a land where the rocks are iron and you can dig copper out of the hills. When you have eaten and are satisfied, praise the Lord your God for the good land he has given you. Be careful that you do not forget the Lord your God, failing to observe his commands, his laws and his decrees that I am giving you this day.

Here we find similar words describing God's abundant provision. Phrases like "you will lack nothing" and "when you have eaten and are satisfied" simply state this truth in a different way. When you "are satisfied" means you have more than enough food to satisfy your appetite. It means a smorgasbord, an all-you-can-eat buffet! It signifies you have food left over. This is the pattern that God wishes to establish for us if we will let Him. As God challenges and changes our belief system, our thinking will change. If our thinking changes about finances, our actions will change.

Obedience is essential

Let's pause for a moment to underline something. In the last passage of scripture (Deuteronomy 8), I have included verse six and verse eleven. Both of these verses speak about obedience to God's Word and by implication obedience to his will. The Lordship of Jesus Christ is foundational for what this book is teaching. Lordship is the key to everything in the Bible. No biblical principle, prosperity or otherwise, works properly without the Lordship of Jesus. It is the key to everything in the Bible. He is Lord of the universe and our wills must always surrender to his. Period!

What is "blessing"?

If we look at Deuteronomy 28, we find both Lordship and prosperity. The first verses speak to fully obeying God (Lordship) and the verses that follow define God's blessings. Let's study this together.

If you fully obey the Lord your God and carefully follow all his commands I give you today, the Lord your God will set you high above all the nations on earth. All these blessings will come upon you and accompany you if you obey the Lord your God: You will be blessed in the city and blessed in the country.

The fruit of your womb will be blessed, and the crops of your land and the young of your livestock— the calves of your herds and the lambs of your flocks. Your basket and your kneading trough will be blessed. You will be blessed when you come in and blessed when you go out. The Lord will grant that the enemies who rise up against you will be defeated before you. They will come at you from one direction but flee from you in seven. The Lord will send a blessing on your barns and on everything you put your hand to. The Lord your God will bless you in the land he is giving you. The Lord will establish you as his holy people, as he promised you on oath, if you keep the commands of the Lord your God and walk in his ways. Then all the peoples on earth will see that you are called by the name of the Lord, and they will fear you. The Lord will grant you abundant prosperity—in the fruit of your womb, the young of your livestock and the crops of your ground—in the land he swore to your forefathers to give you. The Lord will open the heavens, the storehouse of his bounty, to send rain on your land in season and to bless all the work of your hands. You will lend to many nations but will borrow from none. The Lord will make you the head, not the tail. If you pay attention to the commands of the Lord your God that I give you this day and carefully follow them, you will always be at the top, never at the bottom. Do not turn aside from any of the commands I give you today, to the right or to the left, following other gods and serving them (Deuteronomy 28:1–14).

If you obey the Lord, all these blessings will come upon you and accompany you. He will grant you abundant prosperity. The Lord will open the heavens to send rain on your land. If you lend to many and borrow from none, that means you have more money than what you could use for your physical needs. You have surplus to make available to others. God's intention for the children of Israel was blessing, prosperity, freedom and healing. In many ways it is parallel to what we found earlier in 3 John 2. This is blessing. This is God's heart for us.

What is "curse"?

Now that we have defined from the Bible what "blessing" is, let's look at what the Bible says "curse" is. Curse is defined in the next few verses in Deuteronomy 28. What we are going to find is that poverty is included in the list of curses.

However, if you do not obey the Lord your God and do not carefully follow all his commands and decrees I am giving you today, all these curses will come upon you and overtake you.

You will be pledged to be married to a woman, but another will take her and ravish her. You will build a house, but you will not live in it. You will plant a vineyard, but you will not even begin to enjoy its fruit.

You will sow much seed in the field but you will harvest little, because locusts will devour it. You will plant vineyards and cultivate them but you will not drink the wine or gather the grapes, because worms will eat them.

The alien who lives among you will rise above you higher and higher, but you will sink lower and lower. He will lend to you, but you will not lend to him. He will be the head, but you will be the tail.

Because you did not serve the Lord your God joyfully and gladly in the time of prosperity, therefore in hunger and thirst, in nakedness and dire poverty, you will serve the enemies the Lord sends against you. He will put an iron yoke on your neck until he has destroyed you (Deuteronomy 28:15, 30, 38–39, 43–44, 47–48).

We are biblically defining blessings and curses. We find that prosperity is a blessing from God and poverty is a curse from the enemy. We are laying this out as two very clear, distinct, mutually exclusive, separate definitions. This might seem elementary to some, but some Christians get confused about this and start to think that it is more spiritual to be poor and in lack. How can this be when we just read that poverty and lack are the results of disobedience and not obeying the Lord? We must allow the Bible to define these terms for us.

Elisha and the widow

When Elisha helped the widow of one of his prophets with financial provision, he instructed her to gather as many containers as she could find for the oil that was going to be poured out.[1] The oil only stopped flowing when she ran out of containers. Her expectation of God's blessing coincided with how much she received. This is a familiar Bible story, but here again is this principle of more than enough. How much oil did she have? She had more than enough, more than she had containers to fill.

Jehosaphat's plunder

In 2 Chronicles 20, the Lord gave Jehosaphat the victory over Moab and Amman. With his enemies defeated, he advanced to acquire the spoils. When Jehoshaphat and his men attempted to carry off their plunder—a great amount of equipment and clothing and articles of value—it was more than they could carry. In fact, there was so much that it took three days to collect it.

Look for the overflow

In Psalm 23, I read that "I shall not want" and "my cup will be overflowing." If my cup is overflowing means there is more than enough to fill it. Sometimes I joke with people that they need to be careful if I am pouring a drink for them at a social gathering. I am getting such a revelation of more than enough, I just might keep pouring after it is full and overflow their cup. We find the same thing in Proverbs.

Honor the Lord with your wealth, with the firstfruits of all your crops; then your barns will be filled
to overflowing, and your vats will brim over with new
wine (Proverbs 3:9–10).

Overflowing barns? Remember Joseph who had the overflowing crops for seven years as the minister of agriculture in Egypt?
He saved up enough to last for the next seven years of drought. I
recall Jesus talking about a guy that had his barns overflowing in
the New Testament. In both cases the barns were overflowing, but
there was a different use for the surplus on each occasion. What
do we do with the surplus? This is the question we must ask!
Brimming over? This sounds a lot like what we read in Psalm 23
where cups were overflowing. An overflow of new wine sounds
like a good thing to me.

Let's finish our Bible study searching for El Shaddai in the
Old Testament by looking at the book of Malachi.

"Bring the whole tithe into the storehouse, that
there may be food in my house. Test me in this,"
says the Lord Almighty, "and see if I will not throw
open the floodgates of heaven and pour out so much
blessing that you will not have room enough for it.
I will prevent pests from devouring your crops, and
the vines in your fields will not cast their fruit," says
the Lord Almighty. "Then all the nations will call you
blessed, for yours will be a delightful land," says the
Lord Almighty (Malachi 3:10–12).

The Lord promises to pour out so much blessing that we will not have room for it. Here again we find the God-of-more-than-enough! I want to solidly establish the fact that the scripture teaches God to be the God of more than enough. The scripture must be our foundation and our guide.

Is this too good to be true? Does God really want to bless us and our families with more than enough money to do all that he has put in our hearts? Sometimes people have difficulty believing that God loves them that much. As I have been teaching what the Bible shows us in the area of financial prosperity, people sometimes ask if this is just an Old Testament thing. After all, was not the revelation of El Shaddai an Old Testament revelation to Abraham and the children of Israel?

I understand the question because almost everything we have looked at so far has been from the Old Testament. I agree. If what I am teaching about the nature of God is valid, it must appear as a theme throughout the whole Bible. These truths do appear numerous times in the New Testament in the ministry of Jesus and Paul. Let us first take a look at a familiar Bible story.

> As evening approached, the disciples came to him [Jesus] and said, "This is a remote place, and it's already getting late. Send the crowds away, so they can go to the villages and buy themselves some food."
>
> Jesus replied, "They do not need to go away. You give them something to eat."
>
> "We have here only five loaves of bread and two fish," they answered.

"Bring them here to me," he said. And he directed the people to sit down on the grass. Taking the five loaves and the two fish and looking up to heaven, he gave thanks and broke the loaves. Then he gave them to the disciples, and the disciples gave them to the people. They all ate and were satisfied, and the disciples picked up twelve basketfuls of broken pieces that were left over. The number of those who ate was about five thousand men, besides women and children (Matthew 14:15–22).

In this story of the feeding of the five thousand, it states that they all ate enough food and were satisfied. This is how God wants to feed his people—more than they can eat with extra left over. In this case, it was twelve baskets of food that were left over.

Was there money to feed the five thousand?

I also find it interesting to examine the disciples' response when Jesus told them, "You give them something to eat," as recorded by Mark in his gospel. Here is Mark's account:

But he answered, "You give them something to eat."

They said to him, "That would take eight months of a man's wages! Are we to go and spend that much on bread and give it to them to eat?" (Mark 6:37).

The disciples did not say the money was not available to them. In fact, none of the gospel records say they could not afford to buy the food. Let's look at Luke's account of the same incident:

He replied, "You give them something to eat."

They answered, "We have only five loaves of bread and two fish ... unless we go and buy food for all this crowd" (Luke 9:13).

It seems as if they may have had finances available to them, but were concerned about how to use the money available to them. None of us were there, so we do not know for sure. To their credit maybe they would rather have used the money to help the poor. This might be a new way of looking at this Bible story for you, but please consider what these scriptures actually say.

Jesus' ministry

Let us examine another account in Jesus' ministry of more than enough. One day as Jesus was teaching from a fishing boat, he wanted to make a practical example for everyone to understand. We find the story told by Luke in his gospel.

When he had finished speaking, he said to Simon, "Put out into deep water, and let down the nets for a catch."

Simon answered, "Master, we've worked hard all night and haven't caught anything. But because you say so, I will let down the nets." When they had done so, they caught such a large number of fish that their nets began to break. So they signaled their partners in the other boat to come and help them, and they came and filled both boats so full that they began to sink (Luke 5:4–8).

Fishing was the disciples' job. It was how they earned their living. They were not out fishing all night long for a Bible lesson! No, they needed money for their daily provision.

Jesus more than met their financial need. If the fish catch of that day was so big that the nets began to break, and it was so big that it overfilled both boats to the point of sinking, it was definitely more than what they were expecting. Traditionally, most of us have only looked at the later verse where Jesus said the disciples would become fishers of men as the significant spiritual truth taught here. While it is absolutely true that Jesus was teaching this, we cannot overlook the fact that Jesus provided more than enough money for the disciples' paycheck that week. He taught and modeled more than enough.

The parable of the rich man

Earlier we discussed how we should pray and believe for more than enough finances and then ask God what to do with the surplus. Luke records Jesus sharing a parable of a man that did not know what to do with the more than enough that God had provided for him. Let's read that story.

And he told them this parable: "The ground of a certain rich man produced a good crop. He thought to himself, 'What shall I do? I have no place to store my crops.' "Then he said, 'This is what I'll do. I will tear down my barns and build bigger ones, and there I will store all my grain and my goods. And I'll say to myself, "You have plenty of good things laid up for many years. Take life easy; eat, drink and be merry."'

"But God said to him, 'You fool! This very night
your life will be demanded from you. Then who will
get what you have prepared for yourself?' "This is
how it will be with anyone who stores up things for
himself but is not rich toward God" (Luke 12:16–21).

In this parable Jesus never rebuked the man for having more
than enough. In fact, he gave no indication that this is not the
normal pattern. He was teaching about what to do with the surplus that God so graciously provides for us. The rich man in the
parable moved right out of living the life of faith and giving and
moved into self-preservation, materialism and greed. He did not
realize that it was prosperity with a purpose. He did not realize
there was a reason for the surplus he was experiencing.

Remember, giving is the very thing that breaks the power of
money as an idol in our lives. So, by hoarding it, the rich man
actually was empowering money to become a god in his life. He
had no knowledge of what to do with the more than enough.

We find the same idea underlined in Psalm 49. For those of
us with a poverty mindset, our thoughts will automatically apply
this scripture to wealthy non-Christians. We do not see ourselves
as growing rich, and we would likely be "awed" if it happened.
Let us read the following scriptures:

Do not be overawed when a man grows rich, when
the splendor of his house increases; for he will take
nothing with him when he dies, his splendor will not
descend with him.

A man who has riches without understanding is
like the beasts that perish (Psalm 49:16–17, 20).

While this is certainly true for non-Christians, if it is a biblical truth, it should apply to all people, including Christians. We should expect God to bless us financially, but we must understand why he is blessing us. It is for his kingdom. It is to use!

Unlike the rich man in Jesus' parable, King David knew the purpose of his abundance. He was experiencing an abundant level of provision from the Lord, but he knew it was not just for him.

> After David was settled in his palace, he said to Nathan the prophet, "Here I am, living in a palace of cedar, while the ark of the covenant of the Lord is under a tent" (1 Chronicles 17:1).

David knew there was something that was not right about this situation. He found that he was provided for, but God's work was not. He saw his personal house was prosperous, but the Lord's house was desolate. He knew inherently in his heart that this was not acceptable. He knew there was a reason for his prosperity.

Paul's ministry

The apostle Paul did not shrink back from teaching on finances either. He wrote the following instructions to the church at Corinth.

> So I thought it necessary to urge the brothers to visit you in advance and finish the arrangements for the generous gift you had promised. Then it will be ready as a generous gift, not as one grudgingly given. Remember this: Whoever sows sparingly will also reap sparingly, and whoever sows generously will also

reap generously. Each man should give what he has decided in his heart to give, not reluctantly or under compulsion, for God loves a cheerful giver. And God is able to make all grace abound to you, so that in all things at all times, having all that you need, you will abound in every good work. As it is written: "He has scattered abroad his gifts to the poor; his righteousness endures forever." Now he who supplies seed to the sower and bread for food will also supply and increase your store of seed and will enlarge the harvest of your righteousness. You will be made rich in every way so that you can be generous on every occasion, and through us your generosity will result in thanksgiving to God (2 Corinthians 9:5–11).

There is a lot of financial truth for us in this passage of scripture. Let's take a careful look at the content of verse eight, "God is able to make all grace abound to you, so that in all things at all times, having all that you need, you will abound in every good work." Having all that you need sounds like having your needs met and abounding in every good work sounds like giving to others after your needs are met. Combining these two thoughts gives us another biblical example of God's desire to bless us with more than enough. To say these scriptures are not referring to money, as some have done, is blatantly taking this passage out of context.

Paul goes on to tell us that God will provide seed to the sower, not to the stingy one who is trying to hold on, hoard and protect what they have. God will add to the one who is generously giving of what they have, lavishly spreading seed in all directions.

Proverbs chapter eleven, verse 25 states the man who refreshes others is refreshed himself.

Paul's experience

Paul himself never seemed to suffer lack. He always traveled in the most modern form of transportation that was available in his day. It is never recorded in scripture that Paul could not get a boat to the next town because he did not have enough money. The biblical record shows that the Lord directed him to go, and he went. He had the resources that were needed for him to obey God. It was just like Noah, who had the resources he needed to obey God when he was instructed to build the ark.

Acts 24:26 says that the governor Felix sent for Paul frequently and talked with him, hoping that Paul would offer a bribe. Why would the governor Felix, a wealthy man, think that Paul would offer him a bribe? Could it be that Paul had enough money for a bribe large enough to impress Felix?

It is for all believers

If you are still not convinced this truth is found throughout the whole Bible, how about a scripture in the New Testament that states the blessings of Abraham are for the believers of the New Covenant.

> Christ redeemed us from the curse of the law by becoming a curse for us, for it is written: "Cursed is everyone who is hung on a tree." He redeemed us in order that the blessing given to Abraham might come to the Gentiles through Christ Jesus, so that by faith

we might receive the promise of the Spirit (Galatians 3:13–14).

There it is. By faith the blessings given to Abraham are available to both the Jew and the Gentile and also the promise of the Holy Spirit right now as New Testament Christians.

Through Christ, we become heirs of Abraham's blessing. All of the promises of blessing from the Old Testament and the promise of the Holy Spirit are for those who believe, those who are Christians. The Holy Spirit is our teacher. He teaches us to prosper.

We get a total picture of God's heart for us in these scriptures. The church is the seed of Abraham. It is still true today—this is the Father's heart for prosperity and blessings for his children.

APPENDIX B

Portrait of a Typical Millionaire

Lavish lifestyles of the rich and famous? No, the portrait of the average millionaire in America shows anything but this ...

1. Is age 57, a male, married with three children.
2. Most were not millionaires until after fifty years of age.
3. Two-thirds are self-employed in a business.
4. Most are involved in a normal business like plumbing.
5. Their average annual income is $247,000.
6. Their average net worth is $3.7 million.
7. Their average property value is $320,000.
8. Most are first generation affluent: eighty-one percent did not inherit their wealth.
9. Most live below their means and wear inexpensive suits and drive U.S. made cars.
10. Most have enough money saved to live ten years without working.
11. Most attended public school; however their children attend private school.
12. They still work forty-five to fifty-five hours per week.
13. They invest about 20 percent of taxable income each year.
14. Most millionaires do not drive luxury cars and most luxury car drivers are not millionaires.
15. Only half of millionaires live in high status neighborhoods.
16. Thirty percent of millionaires have JC Penney's charge cards and 43 percent have a Sears charge card.

Compiled from *Millionaire Next Door,* Thomas J. Stanley, Ph.D., William D. Danko, Ph.D., (Georgia: Longstreet Press, 1996).

APPENDIX C

What About Job?

You may have noticed as we were looking at the scriptures from the Old Testament regarding prosperity, we did not look at the book of Job. While this is true, it may not be for the reason you might think. There are many valuable lessons in this book of the Bible. In this chapter we will take a careful look at Job, but let's start first in Matthew chapter six. The lesson here is on worry—worry versus faith.

> Therefore I tell you, do not worry about your life, what you will eat or drink; or about your body, what you will wear. Is not life more important than food, and the body more important than clothes? Look at the birds of the air; they do not sow or reap or store away in barns, and yet your heavenly Father feeds them. Are you not much more valuable than they? Who of you by worrying can add a single hour to his life? (Matthew 6:25–27).

Let's briefly focus on the birds of the air. Do they have enough to eat? If you think about it in the natural, physical sense, you would have to answer, "Yes they do." Generally, birds have more than enough to eat. They have all the seeds, bugs, worms and whatever else they need to be well nourished and survive. The only exception is during seasons of drought when there may be a shortage of food. Let's keep reading.

And why do you worry about clothes? See how the lilies of the field grow. They do not labor or spin. Yet I tell you that not even Solomon in all his splendor was dressed like one of these. If that is how God clothes the grass of the field, which is here today and tomorrow is thrown into the fire, will he not much more clothe you, O you of little faith? So do not worry, saying, "What shall we eat?" or "What shall we drink?" or "What shall we wear?" For the pagans run after all these things, and your heavenly Father knows that you need them. But seek first his kingdom and his righteousness, and all these things will be given to you as well. Therefore do not worry about tomorrow, for tomorrow will worry about itself. Each day has enough trouble of its own (Matthew 6:28–34).

Do you think that Solomon had enough of clothes to wear as the king of Israel? In 1 Kings 10:14 it states that King Solomon's income was about 250 tons of gold per year. What is the present dollar value of an ounce of gold? It is somewhere around $1,500 per ounce at the time of this writing. (You can do the math).

If Solomon measured his income in tons of gold per year, it would appear like the King had more than enough clothing! When Solomon went out to battle, he might not have had his whole wardrobe available but it was only for a short time; he generally had more than enough clothes.

Jesus is talking about physical, natural provision here. He did not use John the Baptist, who only had camel's hair to wear, as his example. He could have, but instead he used Solomon as an example.

Dry seasons

Let's look at the book of Job in context. It is about a season of suffering and dryness in Job's life. The lessons in Job are extremely valuable and the Bible would be incomplete without it. There are dry seasons when God is doing something in our lives to make our roots grow deeper into him, and we need to discern and persevere our way through these times of drought. Many times pastors and spiritual leaders will help us through these tough, dry times. Just like the birds of the air suffer lack of food during an occasional drought, Christians also experience seasons of lack in their lives. But as we will see from examining Job's experience, the general pattern of God's provision is one of abundance.

In the beginning of the book of Job, it is important to point out that God blessed Job with many financial and material blessings. It was only after the devil came on the scene that God's blessings were interrupted. It was when Job was under the attack of the devil that he was poor, sick and experiencing calamity. This is what the Bible teaches us. Sometimes, Christians get confused about this and think Job is teaching we should be poor and sick. Just the opposite is true. The book of Job is the story of how a man overcame the attack of the devil and what he learned in the process.

The entire book of Job is about a brief season in his life. Although the Bible does not specifically say, most Bible scholars believe the whole book covers a time span of between three and eighteen months. In the first few chapters, it talks about the day his cattle and servants were lost. While he was still listening to that report another messenger came in stating his sheep were lost and the shepherds killed. And while he was listening to the sheep report, another messenger came and told him his camels were lost. Finally, while Job was listening to the camel report another messenger came and informed Job that his sons and daughters had been killed. All of this in the same day! And we think we have had some bad days?

His situation grew even worse. The next day, Job himself was physically attacked with sickness. All of this transpired in only two days. I am following Job's losses day by day to underline my point that the time of testing for him was a relatively short period of his life.

The rest of the story

If we look at the end of Job it states that he lived 140 years enjoying the blessings of God in every way. The Bible teaches that Job lived most of his life full of prosperity and God's financial provision. Perhaps this is a new way of looking at this Bible story for you. Actually looking at the scripture will help us to see this point more clearly.

> After Job had prayed for his friends, the Lord made him prosperous again and gave him twice as much as he had before. All his brothers and sisters and everyone who had known him before came and ate with him in his house. They comforted and consoled him over all the trouble the Lord had brought upon him, and each one gave him a piece of silver and a gold ring. The Lord blessed the latter part of Job's life more than the first. He had fourteen thousand sheep, six thousand camels, a thousand yoke of oxen and a thousand donkeys. And he also had seven sons and

three daughters. The first daughter he named Jemimah, the second Keziah and the third Keren-Happuch. Nowhere in all the land were there found women as beautiful as Job's daughters, and their father granted them an inheritance along with their brothers. After this, Job lived a hundred and forty years; he saw his children and their children to the fourth generation. And so he died, old and full of years (Job 42:10-17).

Job did not experience one-hundred-forty years of having boils, poverty, despair and everything going wrong. No, it was a short season of his life in which he learned many valuable lessons. Job's story allows us to learn many theological and doctrinal lessons about the nature and character of God. His actual time of testing was much like the occasional drought that causes the birds of the air to experience insufficient food supplies. The example of Job's perseverance is one we can all honor and duplicate.

Job maintains his integrity

The Bible declares that Job maintained his integrity throughout this time of testing. If we are blessed financially, why should we be scared that God's blessing would corrupt or contaminate us? Job is a great example of someone who did not allow his financial status in life, good or bad, to affect his character and integrity.

APPENDIX D

Comparing God's Blessings with His Miracles

Blessings	Miracles
El-Shaddai	Jehovah-Jireh
More than enough	God provides our needs
Sowing and reaping in the Promised Land	Daily manna in the desert
Divine health	Miracles of healing
Divine prosperity	Miracles of provision
Keeps crisis from coming	Deliverance in crisis
God works with you	God works for you
Reliable car that starts all the time	Miracle needed to start the car each day
Your surplus becomes another's miracle	Need met and no extra left over
Blessings have seeds contained in them to plant	No seed to plant

APPENDIX E

Net Worth Worksheet

Name(s)_____

Date _____

My Assets

Present Value

1. Home _____
2. Automobile #1 _____
3. Automobile #2 _____
4. Furnishings (resale) _____
5. Investments
   Stocks _____
   Bonds _____
   CDs_____
   403(b) _____
   IRA #1 _____
   IRA #2 _____
   Mutual Funds _____
   Valuables _____
   Life Insurance cash value_____
   Other _____
6. Cash on Hand _____
7. Checking Account Balance _____
8. Savings Account Balance_____
9. Money Market Funds_____
10. Real Estate Investment (not home) _____
11. Business _____
12. Recreation Equipment (resale)_____
13.. Other_____

   _____

   _____

Total Assets _____

My Liabilities

1. Home Mortgage _____
2. Auto Loan #1 _____
3. Auto Loan #2 _____
4. Credit Card #1 _____
5. Credit Card #2 _____
6. Other Loans _____
7. Unpaid Taxes _____
8. Bills Due_____
9. Other Liabilities _____

_____

Total Liabilities _____
Total Net Worth _____
(Total Assets minus Total Liabilities)

My net worth _____

You can find a realistic value for your vehicle(s) at www.kbb.com or www.nadaguides.com. If you have bought expensive furniture or jewelry, it is worth, at the most, one half of what you have paid for it.

APPENDIX F

Financial Plan Worksheet

Date_____

My plan to change my net worth is as follows:

1. _____
2. _____
3. _____
4. _____
5. _____
6. _____
7. _____
8. _____
9. _____
10. _____

It is best to implement and change only one or two things at a time.
Immediate Changes:
(Example. Buy five shares of stock)

1. _____
2. _____
3. _____

Changes to make six months from now

1. _____
2. _____

Changes to make/ideas to try…

Year One _____

Year Two _____

Year Three _____

Year Four_____

Year Five _____

Year Ten _____

Year 15 _____

Year 25 _____

How much money do I want to sow into the kingdom of God on an annual basis? Remember, giving only starts after you have tithed.

How much money do I want to give to my children?

What are the kinds of kingdom initiatives I would like to give to?

1. _____

2. _____

3. _____

Signature (s) _____

Do not sign this document now. Pick one person who could develop into a long-term financial mentor and ask them for input. You might feel embarrassed to do this, but do it anyway. It will provide accountability.

APPENDIX G

How Can I Find God?

The famous question was asked a long time ago, "What is truth?" In response to Pilate's age-old question, the Bible, God's inspired and true word,[1] is clear that *Jesus is Truth*. To be a Christian means you establish your life on the truth of Jesus. Jesus Himself said, "I am the way and the truth and the life. No one comes to the Father except through me."[2] The Bible reveals a God who seeks us because he longs for intimacy with us. He wants to have a personal relationship with us and be our closest friend.[3] God took the initiative to reveal himself in Jesus Christ.[4]

■ Our problem: separation from God

From the beginning, God created humans to live in unbroken relationship with him, but the first human beings rebelled against God, something we often call *sin*.[5] From that point onward, mankind's vibrant relationship with God was broken. Death entered... but God would not leave us to die separated from his presence.[6] He provided a way to renew the relationship by dealing with the sin issue.

■ God's solution—Jesus

God took the initiative to reveal himself and rescue us through his son, Jesus Christ. God loved us so much he didn't want to see us die in our sin. The Bible says that "... he gave his only Son, so that everyone who believes in him will not perish but have eternal life."[7] So, God sent Jesus to the earth 2,000 years ago, and Jesus took on a human body, lived a perfect life, proclaimed to be God and then suffered and died on a cross, taking on himself the consequences of our moral failures. Although we cannot understand exactly how, God said my sins and your sins were laid upon Jesus when he died on the cross in our place.[8] He became our substitute, and now God does not count our sins against us. In other words, Jesus traded places with us, standing in our place before God for the moral wrong we have done in our lives. In this way Jesus cleared our way back to God while he took the penalty for sin upon himself. He bore our shame in our place. He paid our debt so we could go free.[9]

■ Our response

Everyone comes to God in the same way. We must recognize we are sinners, "For all have sinned; all fall short of God's glorious standard"[10] and repent of our sins, "... if we confess our sins to him, he is faithful and just to forgive us and to cleanse us from every wrong."[11] When we receive Jesus, by faith, God gives us this promise, "... to all who believed him and accepted him, he gave the right to become children of God."[12]

■ Will you trust Jesus Christ as your Lord, giving him control of your life?

Do you see God's great love for you? Do you see your need for his forgiveness? All sin separates you from God. No one is good enough to get to heaven on their own. If you yield your life to Jesus Christ by believing in him and turning away from your sins, he will save you from spiritual death. He died and rose from the dead to set you free. God will transform you from the inside out. He wants to be your friend, a real personal presence who will satisfy the deepest hunger of your heart. Jesus said, speaking figuratively,

"I am the bread of life. No one who comes to me will ever be hungry again. Those who believe in me will never thirst."[13] By asking Jesus—God's son—to forgive you as you decide to follow and obey him, you will discover the purpose for which God created you. There is no other religion, philosophy, or person who can do this but Jesus. He said, "I am the way, the truth, and the life. No one can come to the Father except through me."[14]

Pray this prayer to become a Christian

"God, I know my sins have separated me from you. I am truly sorry, and I want to turn away from my wrongdoing toward you. I believe that your son, Jesus Christ died, for my sins, paying the penalty and bearing my shame so I can be truly free. I invite you, Jesus, to become the Lord of my life, to live in my heart from this day forward. Amen."

In a Nutshell...

The problem

We have all sinned, and are separated from God (Ecclesiastes 7:20; Romans 3:10-12, 23; Isaiah 64:6).

God's solution

God loved you so much; he didn't want to see you die in your sin. "... he does not want anyone to perish, so he is giving more time for everyone to repent" (2 Peter 3:9).

So God gave his only Son, and through his death on the cross, everyone who believes in him will have eternal life (John 3:16; 2 Corinthians 5:19; Colossians 1:22).

Our response

Confess with your mouth, "Jesus is Lord," and believe in your heart that God raised him from the dead, and you will be saved (Romans 10:9-10).

Receive Jesus

To all who believe him and accept him, he gives the right to become children of God (John 1:12).

Footnotes

1   2 Timothy 3:16
2   John 14:6
3   1 John 4:9
4   1John 4:10
5   Romans 3:23
6   2 Peter 3:9
7   John 3:16
8   2 Corinthians 5:19
9   1 Peter 3:18
10   Romans 3:23
11   1 John 1:9
12   John 1:12
13   John 6:35
14   John 14:6

About the author

Initially trained as an industrial engineer at Penn State University, Brian Sauder now provides others with the tools they need to fulfill their God given destiny. Brian has more than 25 years experience in leadership in churches, government and business. Much of his time is spent in leadership training, consulting and development. His book, *A Practical Path to a Prosperous Life,* was birthed out of a personal revelation that has since become a life message.

Brian serves on DOVE International's Apostolic Leadership Council and directs the DOVE Training Schools. Brian has been married to his wife, Janet, for 25 years and they have five children. They provide oversight and direction for churches in Canada, United States and South Africa.

Brian co-authored *The Biblical Role of Elder*s and *Youth Cells and Youth Ministry*. He also compiled *Helping You Build Cell Churches*, a comprehensive training manual for pastors, cell leaders and church planters.

Brian's blog

Read Brian's blog at www.futurenhope.com.

Prosperous Life presentations

For seminars, retreats or other speaking engagements, contact Brian at the DOVE International Offices
11 Toll Gate Road, Lititz, PA 17543
(717) 627-1996 or email BrianS@dcfi.org

For copies of Brian's books

Visit h2hp.com for copies of all of Brian's books.

Other books by Brian Sauder

Helping You Build Cell Churches

A complete biblical blueprint for small group ministry, this manual covers 54 topics! Gives full, integrated training to build cell churches from the ground up. *Compiled by Brian Sauder and Larry Kreider, 224 pages.* **$19.95**

Biblical Role of Elders for Today's Church

New Testament leadership principles for equipping elders. What elders' qualifications and responsibilities are, how they are chosen, how elders are called to be armor bearers, spiritual fathers and mothers, resolving conflicts, and more. *by Larry Kreider, Ron Myer, Steve Prokopchak, Brian Sauder. 278 pages.* **$12.99**

Youth Cells and Youth Ministry

God's heart is expressed for the postmodern generations in the relationship and trust that is provided by youth cell groups. A safe place is provided to learn, discuss, cry, get healed, develop gifts and reach out. This book gives revealing insights into today's youth culture, along with the specifics of implementing cell ministry. Includes a cell leader's job description, creative ideas for youth cells, ministry from junior high to young adults, and how to transition to youth cells. *by Brian Sauder and Sarah Mohler 120 pages.* **$8.50**

**For more resources, seminar details and to order
visit www.dcfi.org**
call 1.800.848.5892   Email: info@dcfi.org